TRIALS IN COLLECTIONS

An Index to Famous Trials
Throughout the World

BY JOHN M. ROSS

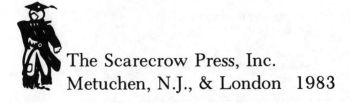

The Scarecrow Press, Inc.
Metuchen, N.J., & London   1983

Library of Congress Cataloging in Publication Data

Ross, John M. (John Murray)
    Trials in collections.

    Bibliography: p.
    1. Trials--Indexes. I. Title.
K546.R67 1983   345'.02   82-21635
ISBN 0-8108-1603-2   342.52

Acknowledgments:

I wish to express my utmost appreciation to Christine Caldwell, Inter-Library Loans Assistant at Cal State University, Los Angeles, for the excellent service she provided in obtaining so many of the "sources" used for this publication.

I would also like to thank Diane Reynolds, Head Reference Librarian, Los Angeles County Law Library, and her staff for their excellent service and cooperation.

CONTENTS

Introduction   vii

List of Abbreviations   xiii

Part I: The Sources   3

Part II: The Defendants; or, Popular Name of Trial   31

Part III: The Offense; or, Subject of Trial

       1: Subject List of Offenses and
          Subjects of Trials   103

       2: The Offense--Classified Under
          Subjects in Subject List   105

       3: Miscellaneous--Offenses that
          Could Not Be Classified Under
          Standard Subjects   200

Bibliography   203

The trials listed here are all famous cases and all have attained notoriety for a variety of reasons, whether they be the persons involved (nobility, prominent citizens, public officials); the magnitude or perverseness of the offense; or landmarks in the history of justice. Whatever their "claim to fame," all are important in varying degrees.

As for the literature itself, TRIALS IN COLLECTIONS indexes principally compilations of trials in the English language that were cited in the Library of Congress Subject Catalog, the British National Bibliography, and the Cumulative Book Index, from 1950 through 1980. An effort has been made to index only those titles that deal almost exclusively with the trials themselves, including reconstructed accounts of the trials, rather than with the character of individual defendants, the political climate in which the trial occurred, or the offense involved. Also excluded were collections that presented only a brief statement of the trial and fell short of offering any significant contribution to the literature. In view of these selection criteria, it should therefore be understood that this index does not include all collections that appeared in the Library of Congress Subject Catalog, the British National Bibliography, and the Cumulative Book Index.

The index also covers, but within a more limited scope, selected compilations published prior to 1950. Titles for this category were chosen from the Cumulative Book Index, 1900-1950; from the holdings at the Los Angeles County Law Library, the UCLA Research Library, and the UCLA Law Library; and from the various bibliographic sources I encountered during the course of my research--these include many of the indexed titles themselves (see list of "Sources"), while the other sources are included in the "Bibliography."

Although TRIALS IN COLLECTIONS is international in

vii

coverage, it is confined to publications in the English language. As a result there is a slant toward cases from the English-speaking world, especially the United States and Great Britain, a point to be kept in mind while making use of this work.

A final point in coverage should be made clear: the index is confined to the "book" literature (nonofficial sources) on trials and does not include any of the judicial opinions reported by the various courts (Supreme Court, federal or national, and state). The opinions can be found through the legal digests, and so there would be no point in duplicating these existing services.

The need for this index

The idea for TRIALS IN COLLECTIONS grew out of my experiences as a reference librarian. I frequently received requests for information about various trials. Unless a trial was famous enough or popular enough to have had a book written about it, the only recourse was to refer patrons to the sections of the library that contained trials in collections where they could thumb through individual titles searching for their particular trial. This often proved to be time consuming and unwieldy, as collections are classified generally, geographically, and by type of offense. Quite frequently the patrons' searches led nowhere because of the lack of an index to collected trials.

My own experiences as well as those of other information specialists in academic, law, public, and secondary school libraries clearly indicated a definite need for an index that would permit easy and quick access to trials in collections. The need has been so great at some libraries that staffs have attempted to maintain individual indexes to trials contained in various collections. Such indexes or card files were limited to collections owned by each library and were rarely kept current. As a result of talking to other librarians, it became even more apparent to me that here was an important area of social history that lacked retrieval. Since no index to this literature existed, I decided to bridge this information gap.

The index serves a variety of uses. Although a few accounts are of monograph size, the index is especially de-

signed for the reader who wants concise, journalistic accounts
of trials rather than the official case reports.   Second, it
serves the reader who is looking just for basic information
on a trial.   Finding a trial account here may often remove
the necessity of ploughing through lengthily documented mono-
graphs or the legalese of case reports.   Third, the index
can be useful for comparing opinions or interpretations on a
particular case--notice the frequency in which certain cases
are cited.   In the case of Oscar Wilde, as late as the 1950s
his offense (or lifestyle) was described as "filthy and disgust-
ing" (Hastings, Famous and Infamous Cases, p. 241. [List
of Sources, no. 129]).   Yet in most Western countries today,
homosexuality between consenting adults is well within the
law.

In addition to serving as an index to trials, the index
itself can be used as a reference book in that it allows read-
ers to search out particular facts or highlights of a case that
are of unique interest to them.   By referring to this index
one can find out the popular names of certain trials and defendants, when and where they took place, and what type of
offense was involved.

Construction and organization of this index

The index is divided into three parts: The Sources, The Defendants, and The Offenses.

In Part I, The Sources, each title indexed is numbered
and listed in alphabetical order.   Each title contained in the
index was analyzed in depth; however, not every single trial
from each collection is indexed due to the uneven coverage in
some of the collections.   For example, some collections might
only contain a page and a half about one trial and a comprehensive account of the next.   All comprehensive accounts were
indexed.   The brief references were excluded from the index
except where there were important sources cited, such as
newspaper accounts, legal opinions, and other bibliographical
references.

In Part II, The Defendants, an attempt has been made
to give as many cross-references as possible to facilitate research.   Such cross-references include name variations, nick-
names, epithets, titles, and other descriptors.   Names of
British nobility are cited as they appear in the Dictionary of

National Biography, titles of persons being cross-referenced
to their family or official name.

        Included here are popular names of trials cross-
referenced from the defendant. For example, a trial may be
better known by a popular or media name rather than by the
name of the defendant. When Dr. Benjamin Spock and four
others were tried for conspiracy, the case became known as
the BOSTON FIVE. This case is therefore indexed under
Boston Five with a cross-reference from Dr. Spock. The
same principle applies to the Army-McCarthy hearings and
Joseph McCarthy, and to the Harrisburg 7 and Philip Berrigan, as well as to all trials readily identified by their popular name. In cases where a trial acquired a popular name
but continued to be more identified with the defendant, then the
trial is cited under the defendant with a cross-reference from
the acquired name. Undoubtedly not everyone will agree as
to what name takes precedence, but the important thing is to
be able to find the case regardless of the choice of entry.

        For civil cases both the defendant and the plaintiff are
cited, as in legal references.

        In Part III, The Offenses, the legal terms given in the
Library of Congress Subject Headings (index) or in Black's
Law Dictionary have been used wherever possible to refer to
each offense. When this was impractical the popular or lay
term has been used and is placed under SUBJECT OF TRIAL.
Scopes, for example, was charged with a misdemeanor, which
is meaningless in a work of this nature. The true subject of
his trial was Evolution in the Schools, and his trial is included under that heading. David Mitchell was charged with
civil disobedience, but the cause of his indictment was draft-
card burning, and the heading under which his case is cited
is Draft Resistance. The caption SUBJECT OF TRIAL also
applied to some civil cases that are included here.

        Related offenses and those that overlap other trans-
gressions of the law are connected by See and See also references similar to those found in the Library of Congress Subject Headings (index).

        Finally, trials are a reflection of the times in which
they occur and to be understood at all must be viewed as a
product of the judicial system and country in which they took
place. For that reason I have supplied two additional pieces

of information: where and when the trial took place.   Compare the handling of a particular offense today with the way
that same offense was handled two hundred years ago.   The
outcome of the conspiracy trials (Vietnam War Protestors)
in the United States is a far cry from the execution sentences
handed down to the conspirators of the 1790s.   But we need
not go back so far to witness these vagaries of justice.   Sim-
ply compare the punishment meted out to Irma Grese for war
crimes in 1945 with that given Lieutenant Calley in 1968.
Miss Grese was tried by the victors and was executed; Calley,
tried by his own country, was found guilty but never sent to
prison.

        And on a matter of very recent interest, many of us
were shocked by the new development in the Leo Frank case.
It was reported (Los Angeles Times, 3/6/82, sec. I, p. 2)
that a witness has come forth and identified the true murderer
of Mary Fagan.   The defendant, Leo Frank, was convicted
and sentenced to death.   His sentence was commuted to life
imprisonment, but some of the citizens were not satisfied
with this and had him lynched.   Frank, as it appears now,
was not the murderer at all, but then Frank was a Jew and
tried in Georgia in 1913.

        The index is expected to provide the most important
information for gaining access to the trials-in-collections
literature.   There are, admittedly, other important elements
of the trials that were not included, but a cut-off had to be
made somewhere.   Here, for example, the plaintiffs, except
for civil cases, were not included, nor were the names of
victims in criminal cases, nor the names of prosecutors, nor
defense attorneys.   There is the odd case where the date of
a trial or the defendant's first name is lacking.   This information could not be found in the sources available to me.
Apart from these minor exceptions, however, all the information that falls within the scope of this index has been provided.

Adm.	Admiral
Bp.	Bishop
c.	circa
Capt.	Captain
Card.	Cardinal
Col.	Colonel
Com.	Commander
Commo.	Commodore
D. A.	District Attorney
ed.	edition, editor
Gen.	General
Gov.	Governor
Lt.	Lieutenant
Maj.	Major
NYC	New York City
P. M.	Prime Minister
Pres.	President
pseud.	pseudonym
pt.	part(s)
Pvt.	Private
Rev.	Reverend
Sen.	Senator
Sgt.	Sergeant
St.	Saint
v.	versus; volume(s)

TRIALS IN COLLECTIONS

1. ADAM, George Jeffreys. Treason and Tragedy; An Account of French War Trials. London: Cape, 1929. 253p.

2. ADAMS, A. K., comp. Favorite Trial Stories; Fact and Fiction. New York: Dodd, Mead, 1966. 402p.

3. ADAMS, Laurie. Art on Trial: From Whistler to Rothko. New York: Walker, ©1976. 236p.

4. AIYAR, R. P. In the Crimelight. Foreword by R. K. Karanjia. Bombay: Pearl; distributed by India Book House, 1967. 173p.

5. ALLES, Anthony Christopher. Famous Criminal Cases of Sri Lanka. Colombo: Colombo Apothecaires' Co., 1977-78. 2v.

6. AMBLER, Eric. The Ability to Kill, and Other Pieces. London: Bodley Head, 1963. 222p.

7. The ANATOMY of Murder; Famous Cases Critically Considered by Members of the Detection Club: Helen Simpson, John Rhode, pseud., and Others. New York: Macmillan, 1937. 335p.

8. ATLAY, James Beresford. Famous Trials of the Century. Chicago: H. S. Stone, 1899. 393p.

9. AVERBACH, Albert, and Charles Price, eds. The Verdicts Were Just; Eight Famous Lawyers Present Their Most Memorable Cases. Rochester, N.Y.: Lawyers Co-operative, 1966. 277p.

3

10.   AYMAR, Brandt, and Edward Sagarin.   Laws and Trials
      That Created History.   New York: Crown, 1974.
      214p.

11.   AYMAR, Brandt, and Edward Sagarin.   A Pictorial His-
      tory of the World's Great Trials, from Socrates to
      Eichmann.   New York: Crown, 1967.   373p.

12.   BAILEY, Francis Lee, with Harvey Aronson.   The De-
      fense Never Rests.   New York: Stein and Day, 1971.
      262p.

13.   BAILEY, Francis Lee, with John Greenya.   For the
      Defense.   New York: Atheneum, 1975.   367p.

14.   BANNAN, John F., and Rosemary S. Bannan.   Law,
      Morality, and Vietnam: The Peace Militants and
      the Courts.   Bloomington: Indiana University Press,
      1974.   241p.

15.   BARDENS, Dennis.   Famous Cases of Norman Birkett,
      X.C.   London: Hale, 1963.   222p.

16.   BARDENS, Dennis.   Lord Justice Birkett.   London:
      Hale, 1962.   288p.

17.   BARKER, Dudley.   Lord Darling's Famous Cases.   Lon-
      don: Hutchinson, 1956.   256p.

18.   BATAILLE, Albert.   Dramas of the French Courts.
      London: Hutchinson, 1941.   288p.
      Also published under title: Inside the French Courts.

19.   BAYER, Oliver Weld (pseud.), ed.   Cleveland Murders,
      by Howard Beaufait, and Others.   New York: Duell,
      Sloan and Pearce, 1947.   249p.   (Regional Murder
      Series, v. 6.)

20.   BELL, Charles William.   Who Said Murder?   Toronto:
      Macmillan, 1935.   403p.

21.   BELTRAMI, Joseph.   The Defenders.   Foreword by
      Nicholas Fairbairn.   Introduction by William Allsopp.
      Edinburgh: Chambers, 1980.   238p.

22.   BENNETT, Benjamin.   ... And Your Verdict?   Cape
      Town: Timmins, 1954.   256p.

23. BENNETT, Benjamin. The Clues Condemn. Cape
      Town: Timmins, 1949. 259p.

24. BENNETT, Benjamin. The Evil That Men Do. Cape
      Town: Timmins, 195?. 237p.

25. BENNETT, Benjamin. Famous South African Murders.
      London: Laurie, 1938. 221p.

26. BENNETT, Benjamin. Murder Is My Business. Cape
      Town: Timmins for Hodder & Stoughton; London:
      Bailey & Swinfen, 1951. 286p.

27. BENNETT, Benjamin. Murder Will Speak. Cape Town:
      Timmins, 1962. 284p.

28. BENNETT, Benjamin. The Noose Tightens. Cape
      Town: Timmins, 1974. 266p.

29. BENNETT, Benjamin. Too Late for Tears. London:
      Hodder & Stoughton, 1948. 234p.

30. BENNETT, Benjamin, in collaboration with François
      Pierre Rousseau. Up for Murder. London: Hutch-
      inson, 1934. 287p.

31. BENNETT, Benjamin. Why Did They Do It? Cape
      Town: Timmins, 1953. 310p.

32. BENNETT, Benjamin. Why Men Kill. Cape Town:
      Timmins, 1965. 186p.

33. BENSON, Captain L., ed. The Book of Remarkable
      Trials and Notorious Characters. From "Half-
      Hanged Smith," 1700-to Oxford Who Shot at the Queen,
      1840.... Illustrated by Phiz (pseud.). London:
      Hotten, 1871. 545p.

34. BIERSTADT, Edward Hale. Curious Trials & Criminal
      Cases from Socrates to Scopes. Garden City, N.Y.:
      Garden City, 1934? 366p.

35. BIERSTADT, Edward Hale. Enter Murderers. Eight
      Studies in Murder. Garden City, N.Y.: Doubleday,
      Doran, 1934. 302p.

36. BIRKENHEAD, Frederick Edwin Smith. Famous Trials

of History. Garden City, N. Y.: Garden City, 1926.
319p.

37. BIRKENHEAD, Frederick Edwin Smith. More Famous
     Trials. Garden City, N. Y.: Doubleday, Doran,
     1929. 298p.

38. BISSET, Ian. Trial at Arms; Some Famous Trials by
     Court Martial. London: MacGibbon & Kee, 1957.
     215p.

39. BLACKBURN, Sara, comp. White Justice; Black Ex-
     perience Today in America's Courtrooms. Foreword
     by Haywood Burns. New York: Harper and Row,
     1971. 289p.

40. BLEACKLEY, Horace William. Some Distinguished Vic-
     tims of the Scaffold. London: Kegan Paul, Trench,
     Trübner, 1905. 232p.

41. BLOCK, Eugene B. The Fabric of Guilt; True Stories
     of Criminals Caught in a Net of Circumstantial Evi-
     dence. Garden City, N. Y.: Doubleday, 1968. 215p.

42. BLOCK, Eugene B. The Vindicators. London: Redman,
     1964. 272p.

43. BODKIN, Matthias McDonnell. Famous Irish Trials.
     Dublin: Maunsel, 1918. 212p.

44. BORROW, George, ed. Celebrated Trials and Remark-
     able Cases of Jurisprudence from the Earliest Rec-
     ords to the Year 1825. Revised and Edited by Ed-
     ward Hale Bierstadt. London: Cape, 1928. 2v.

45. BRENNAN, John. Great Scandals of Cheating at Cards;
     Famous Court Cases, by John Welcome (pseud). New
     York: Horizon, 1963. 235p.

46. BROME, Vincent. Reverse Your Verdict; A Collection
     of Private Prosecutions. London: Hamilton, 1971.
     210p.

47. BROWNE, Douglas Gordon, and E. V. Tullett. The
     Scalpel of Scotland Yard; The Life of Sir Bernard
     Spilsbury. Foreword by W. Bentley Purchase. New
     York: Dutton, 1952. 503p.

48. BROWNE, George Lathom. Narratives of State Trials
     in the Nineteenth Century. First Period. From the
     Union with Ireland to the Death of George the Fourth,
     1801-1830. Boston: Houghton, Mifflin, 1882. 2v.

49. BROWNE, George Lathom, and C. G. Stewart. Reports
     of Trials for Murder by Poisoning; by Prussic Acid,
     Strychnia, Antimony, Arsenic and Aconitia. Including
     the Trials of Tawell, W. Palmer, Dove, Madeline
     Smith, Dr. Pritchard, Smethurst, and Dr. Lamson,
     with Chemical Introduction and Notes on the Poisons
     Used. London: Stevens and Sons, 1883. 604p.

     BRUMBAUGH, Robert S. , ed. see Six Trials

50. BURKE, Peter. Celebrated Naval and Military Trials.
     London: Allen, 1866. 399p.

51. BURKE, Peter. Celebrated Trials Connected with the
     Aristocracy in the Relations of Private Life. London:
     Benning, 1849. 505p.

52. BURKE, Peter. Recollections of the Courtroom; or,
     Narratives, Scenes and Anecdotes from Courts of
     Justice. New York: Dayton, 1859. 308p.
     Also published under title: The Romance of the Forum.

53. BURNABY, Evelyn Henry Villebois. Memories of Fa-
     mous Trials. London: Sisley's, 1907. 231p.

54. BUSCH, Francis Xavier. Casebook of the Curious and
     True. Indianapolis: Bobbs-Merrill, 1957. 228p.

55. BUSCH, Francis Xavier. Enemies of the State; An Ac-
     count of the Trials of the Mary Eugenia Surratt Case,
     the Teapot Dome Cases, the Alphonse Capone Case,
     and the Rosenberg Case. Indianapolis: Bobbs-Mer-
     rill, 1954. 299p. (His Notable American Trials.)

56. BUSCH, Francis Xavier. Guilty or Not Guilty? An Ac-
     count of the Trials of the Leo Frank Case, the D. C.
     Stephenson Case, the Samuel Insull Case, the Alger
     Hiss Case. Indianapolis: Bobbs-Merrill, 1952.
     287p.

57. BUSCH, Francis Xavier. Prisoners at the Bar; An Ac-
     count of the Trials of the William Haywood Case, the

Sacco-Vanzetti Case, the Loeb-Leopold Case, the Bruno Hauptmann Case.   Freeport, N.Y.:   Books for Libraries, 1970, © 1952.   288p.   (Biography Index Reprint Series.)

58.   BUSCH, Francis Xavier.   They Escaped the Hangman: An Account of the Trials of the Caleb Powers Case, the Rice Patrick Case, the Hall-Mills Case, and the Hans Haupt Case.   Indianapolis: Bobbs-Merrill, 1953. 301p.   (His Notable American Trials.)

59.   CALDER-MARSHALL, Arthur.   Arthur Calder-Marshall's Lewd, Blasphemous & Obscene: Being the Trials and Tribulations of Sundry Founding Fathers of To-day's Alternative Societies.   London: Hutchinson, 1972.   248p.

60.   CASEY, Lee Taylor, ed.   Denver Murders, by William E. Barrett, and Others.   New York: Duell, Sloan and Pearce, 1946.   217p.   (Regional Murder Series, v. 3.)

61.   CASSWELL, Joshua David.   A Lance for Liberty.   Foreword by Lord Oaksey.   London: Harrap, 1961. 325p.

CELEBRATED Murders as Shown in Remarkable Capital Trials see MYSTERIES of Crime

62.   CHANDLER, Peleg Whitman.   American Criminal Trials. Freeport, N.Y.:   Books for Libraries, 1970.   2v.

63.   CHARI, A.S.R.   Trials of Strength.   Bombay: Sangam, 1975.   101p.

64.   CHEVIGNY, Paul.   Cops and Rebels: A Study of Provocation.   New York: Pantheon, 1972.   332p.

65.   CHILDERS, Hugh Robert Eardley.   Romantic Trials of Three Centuries; with Twenty-four Illustrations.   London: Lane, 1913.   303p.

66.   CLEGG, Eric.   Return Your Verdict; Some Studies in Australian Murder.   Introduction by Sir John Barry. Sydney: Angus and Robertson, 1965.   204p.

67.   CLINTON, Henry Lauren.   Celebrated Trials.   New York: Harper, 1897.   626p.

68. CLINTON, Henry Lauren. Extraordinary Cases. New
     York: Harper, 1896. 406p.

69. CLUNE, Frank. Scandals of Sydney Town: The Mount
     Rennie Case; the Case of Ernest Buttner; the Dean
     Case; the Coningham Conspiracy; the Land Scandals;
     the Careers of W. P. Crick and R. D. Meagher.
     Illustrated by Virgil Reilly. Sydney, London: Angus
     & Robertson, 1957. 228p.

70. COBB, Belton. Trials and Errors, 11 Miscarriages of
     Justice. London: Allen, 1962. 192p.

71. COCKBURN, Henry Cockburn (Lord). An Examination
     of the Trials for Sedition Which Have Hitherto Oc-
     curred in Scotland. New York: Kelley, 1970. 2v.
     in 1.
     Reprint of 1888 ed.

72. COLLINS, Ted, ed. New York Murders, by Angelica
     Gibbs, and Others. New York: Duell, Sloan and
     Pearce, 1944. 242p. (Regional Murder Series, v.
     1.)

73. CRAIK, George Lillie, ed. English Causes Célèbres; or,
     Reports of Remarkable Trials. Illustrated by the
     author. London: Knight, 1844. 296p.

74. CREW, Albert. The Old Bailey; History, Constitution,
     Functions, Notable Trials. London: Nicholson &
     Watson, 1933. 302p.

75. DAVENPORT, William H., ed. Voices in Court; A
     Treasury of the Bench, the Bar, and the Collection.
     New York: Macmillan, 1958. 588p.

     DAVID, Andrew (pseud.) see WHITTINGHAM, Richard

76. DEALE, Kenneth E. L. Beyond Any Reasonable Doubt?
     A Book of Murder Trials. Dublin: Gill and Mac-
     millan, 1971. 194p.

77. DEALE, Kenneth E. L. Memorable Irish Trials. Lon-
     don: Constable, 1960. 190p.

78. DEANS, Richard Storry. Notable Trials: Difficult Cases.
     London: Chapman and Hall, 1932. 232p.

79. DeFORD, Miriam Allen. Murderers Sane & Mad; Case
     Histories in the Motivation and Rationale of Murder.
     London: Abelard-Schuman, 1965. 239p.

80. DERLETH, August. Wisconsin Murders. Sauk City:
     Mycroft and Moran, 1968. 222p.

81. DEVITT, Napier. Famous South African Trials. Pre-
     toria: van Schaik, 1930. 194p.

     DEWES, Simon (pseud.) see MURIEL, John St. Clair

82. DICKLER, Gerald. Man on Trial; History-Making Trials
     from Socrates to Oppenheimer. Garden City, N. Y. :
     Doubleday, 1962. 452p.

83. DILNOT, George. Rouges' March. London: Bles,
     1934. 240p.

84. DiMONA, Joseph. Great Court-Martial Cases. New
     York: Grosset & Dunlap, 1972. 291p.

85. DORMAN, Michael. King of the Courtroom: Percy Dor-
     man for the Defense. New York: Delacorte, 1969.
     327p.

86. DOUTHWAITE, Louis Charles. Mass Murder. Fore-
     word by George Dilnot. London: Long, 1928. 288p.

87. DuCANN, Charles Garfield Lott. Famous Treason Trials.
     New York: Walker, 1965, © 1964. 272p.
     Also published under title: English Treason Trials.

88. DUKE, Winifred. Six Trials. London: Gollancz, 1934. 287p.

89. DUNPHY, Thomas, and Thomas J. Cummins. Remark-
     able Trials of All Countries; Particularly of the United
     States, Great Britain, Ireland and France: With Notes
     and Speeches of Counsel. Containing Thrilling Narra-
     tives of Fact from the Courtroom, Also Historical
     Reminiscences of Wonderful Events. New York: Di-
     ossy & Cockcroft, 1867-82. 2v.

90. EATON, Harold. Famous Poison Trials. London: Col-
     lins, 1923. 246p.

91. ELDREDGE, L. H. Trials of a Philadelphia Lawyer.
     Philadelphia: Lippincott, 1968. 257p.

92. ERSKINE, Thomas Erskine. Speeches of Lord Erskine,
     While at the Bar. Edited by James L. High. Chica-
     go: Callaghan, 1876. 4v.

93. FAUNTLEROY, Henry. Trial of Henry Fauntleroy, and
     Other Famous Trials for Forgery. Edited by Horace
     Bleackley. Edinburgh: Hodge, 1924. 269p.

94. FELSTEAD, Sidney Theodore. Famous Criminals and
     Their Trials; Intimate Revelations Compiled from the
     Papers of Sir Richard Muir, Late Senior Counsel to
     the British Treasury. Edited by Lady Muir. Illus-
     trated. New York: Doran, 1926. 382p.

95. FEUERBACH, Paul Johann Anselm. Narratives of Re-
     markable Criminal Trials. Translated from the Ger-
     man by Lady Duff Gordon. New York: Harper, 1846.
     339p.

96. FIRMIN, Stanley. Murderers in Our Midst. London:
     Hutchinson, 1955. 192p.

97. FITZGERALD, John D. Studies in Australian Crime.
     Sydney: Cornstalk, 1924. 2v.

98. FLEMING, Alice Mulcahey. Trials That Made Head-
     lines. New York: St. Martin, 1974. 146p.

     FRANKLIN, Charles see USHER, Frank Hugh

99. FULLER, Horace Williams. Noted French Trials; Im-
     posters and Adventurers. Boston: Soule & Bugbee,
     1882. 264p.

100. FURNEAUX, Rupert. Courtroom U. S. A. London: Pen-
     guin, 1962-63. 2v.

101. FURNEAUX, Rupert. Famous Criminal Cases. Lon-
     don: Wingate, 1954-62. 7v.

102. FURNEAUX, Rupert. Tried by Their Peers. London:
     Cassell, 1959. 202p.

103. GAUBA, Khalid Latif. Battles at the Bar. Bombay:
      Tripathi, 1956. 288p.

104. GAUBA, Khalid Latif. Famous and Historical Trials.
      Delhi: Hind Pocket Books, 1972. 186p.

105. GAUBA, Khalid Latif. Famous Trials for Love and
      Murder. Delhi: Hind Pocket Books, 1967. 175p.

106. GAUBA, Khalid Latif. The Pakistani Spy and Other
      Famous Trials. Delhi: Hind Pocket Books, 1968. 176p.

107. GAUBA, Khalid Latif. The Shamim Rahmani Case and
      Other Famous Trials. Delhi: Hind Pocket Books,
      1971. 135p.

108. GLAISTER, John. The Power of Poison. New York:
      Morrow, 1955? 272p.

109. GOODMAN, Derick. Crime of Passion. London: Pan,
      1960. 222p.

110. GOODMAN, Jonathan. Posts-Mortem; The Correspond-
      ence of Murder. New York: St. Martin, 1972. 164p.

      GRAHAM, Evelyn (pseud.) see LUCAS, Netley

111. GRIBBLE, Leonard Reginald. Justice? Stories of Fa-
      mous Modern Trials. New York: Abelard-Schuman,
      1971, © 1970. 160p.
      Also published under title: Stories of Famous Modern
      Trials.

112. GRIBBLE, Leonard Reginald. They Got Away with Mur-
      der. London: Long, 1971. 160p.

113. GRICE, Edward. Great Cases of Sir Henry Curtis
      Bennett. London: Hutchinson, 1937. 156p.

114. GRIERSON, Francis Durham. Famous French Crimes.
      London: Muller, 1959. 216p.

115. GRIMSHAW, Eric, and Glyn Jones. Lord Goddard; His
      Career and Cases. London: Wingate, 1958. 175p.

116. GURR, Tom, and Harry Cox. Famous Australasian
      Crimes. London: Muller, 1957. 192p.

117. HABE, Hans. Gentlemen of the Jury. Translated from
      the German by Frances Hogarth-Gaute. London:
      Harrap, 1967. 268p.

118. HALE, Leslie. Blood on the Scales. London: Cape,
      1960. 223p.

119. HALE, Leslie. Hanged in Error. Baltimore: Penguin,
      1961. 160p.

120. HALE, Leslie. Hanging in the Balance. London: Cape,
      1962. 224p.

121. HALL, Sir John Richard. The Bravo Mystery and Other
      Cases. New York: Dodd, Mead, 1925. 299p.

122. HAMER, Alvin C., ed. Detroit Murders, by Patricia
      Brontë, and Others. New York: Duell, Sloan and
      Pearce, 1948. 218p. (Regional Murder Series, v. 8.)

123. HANNAY, James Owen. Famous Murders. London:
      Chatto & Windus, 1935. 848p.
      Also published under title: Murder Most Foul.

124. HARDWICK, John Michael Drinkrow. Doctors on Trial.
      London: Jenkins, 1961. 192p.

125. HARDWICK, John Michael Drinkrow, ed. The Verdict
      of the Court. Introduction and Summing-up by Lord
      Birkett. London: Jenkins, 1960. 198p.

126. HARRIS, Chester. Tiger at the Bar; The Life Story of
      Charles J. Margiotti. New York: Vantage, 1956.
      452p.

127. HASSARD, Albert Richard. Famous Canadian Trials.
      Toronto: Carswell, 1924. 246p.

128. HASTINGS, Sir Patrick. Cases in Court. London:
      Heinemann, 1949. 342p.

129. HASTINGS, Sir Patrick. Famous and Infamous Cases.
      New York: Roy, 1954? 263p.

130. HAYS, Arthur Garfield. Let Freedom Ring. New York:
      Da Capo, 1972, © 1937. 475p.

131. HAYS, Arthur Garfield. Trial by Prejudice. New
      York: Da Capo, 1970, © 1933. 369p.

132. HICKS, Sir Seymour. Not Guilty M'Lord. London:
      Cassell, 1939. 276p.

133. HILL, Frederick Trevor. Decisive Battles of the Law;
      Narrative Studies of Eight Legal Contests Affecting
      the History of the United States Between the Years
      1800 and 1886. New York: Harper, 1907. 267p.
      Reprinted from Harper's magazine.

134. HISTORY Is My Witness. Foreword by James Cameron.
      Edited by Gordon Menzies. London: British Broad-
      casting Corporation, 1976. 144p.

135. HODGE, Harry, ed. The Black Maria; or, The Crimi-
      nals' Omnibus. London: Gollancz, in association
      with W. Hodge, 1935. 1,012p.

136. HODGE, Harry, ed. Famous Trials. 1st Series. Lon-
      don: Penguin, 1954. 155p.

137. HODGE, Harry, ed. Famous Trials. 2nd Series.
      West Drayton, Middlesex: Penguin, 1948. 222p.

138. HODGE, James Hozier, ed. Famous Trials. 3d Series.
      Harmondsworth, Middlesex: Penguin, 1950. 235p.

139. HODGE, James Hozier, ed. Famous Trials. 4th Se-
      ries. London, Baltimore: Penguin, 1954. 220p.

140. HODGE, James Hozier, ed. Famous Trials. 5th Se-
      ries. Harmondsworth, Middlesex: Penguin, 1955.
      223p.

141. HODGE, James Hozier, ed. Famous Trials. 6th Se-
      ries. Harmondsworth, Middlesex: Penguin, 1962.
      198p.

142. HODGE, James Hozier, ed. Famous Trials. 8th Se-
      ries. Harmondsworth, Middlesex: Penguin, 1963.
      222p.

143. HODGE, James Hozier, ed. Famous Trials. Final
      Selection (10th Series). Baltimore: Penguin, 1964.
      204p.

144.   HOUSE, Brant (pseud.), ed. Great Trials of Famous
        Lawyers. New York: Ace, 1962. 224p.

145.   HOUSE, Jack. Square Mile of Murder. Edinburgh:
        Chambers, 1961. 253p.

146.   HUGGETT, Renée. Daughters of Cain: The Story of
        Nine Women Executed Since Edith Thompson in 1923.
        London: Pan, 1961. 315p.

147.   HUMPHREYS, Christmas. Seven Murderers. London:
        Heinemann, 1931. 292p.

148.   HUSON, Richard, ed. Sixty Famous Trials. Introduc-
        tion by Percy Hoskins. London: Daily Express,
        1938. 876p.

149.   HYDE, Harford Montgomery. Crime Has Its Heroes.
        London: Constable, 1976. 244p.

150.   HYDE, Harford Montgomery, in collaboration with John
        H. Kisch. An International Casebook of Crime. Lon-
        don: Barrie & Rockliff, 1962. 218p.

151.   HYDE, Harford Montgomery. Norman Birkett; The Life
        of Lord Birkett of Ulverston. London: Hamilton,
        1964. 638p.

152.   HYDE, Harford Montgomery. Their Good Names:
        Twelve Cases of Libel and Slander with Some Intro-
        ductory Reflections on the Law. London: Hamilton,
        1970. 406p.

153.   IRVING, Henry Brodribb. A Book of Remarkable Crim-
        inals. New York: Hyperion, 1975, © 1918. 315p.

154.   IRVING, Henry Brodribb. Last Studies in Criminology.
        London: Collins, 1923. 281p.

155.   JACKSON, Joseph Henry, ed. San Francisco Murders,
        by Allan R. Bosworth, and Others. New York: Duell,
        Sloan and Pearce, 1947. 314p. (Regional Murder
        Series, v. 4.)

156.   JACOBS, Philip Acland. Famous Australian Trials and
        Memories of the Law. Foreword by Sir Frederick

Wollaston Mann.   Second Edition.   Melbourne: Robertson & Mullens, 1943.   231p.

157.   JACOBS, Thomas Curtis Hicks.   Aspects of Murder.
       London: Paul, 1956.   224p.
       Also published under title: Pageant of Murder.

158.   JESSE, Fryniwyd Tennyson.   Comments on Cain.   In-
       troduction by Anthony Boucher.   New York: Collier,
       1964.   158p.

159.   JESSE, Fryniwyd Tennyson.   Murder and Its Motives.
       Revised Edition. London: Pan, 1958.   224p.

160.   JOHNSON, Lewis Franklin.   Famous Kentucky Tragedies
       and Trials; A Collection of Important and Interesting
       Tragedies and Criminal Trials Which Have Taken
       Place in Kentucky.   Revised Edition.   Lexington, Ky. :
       Henry Clay, 1972.   336p.

161.   JONES, Elwyn.   On Trial: Seven Intriguing Cases of
       Capital Crime.   Introduction by Lord Elwyn Jones.
       London: Macdonald and Jane, 1978.   160p.

162.   JOWITT, William Allen Jowitt, 1st Earl.   Some Were
       Spies.   London: Hodder and Stoughton, 1954.   223p.

163.   KEETON, George Williams.   Guilty but Insane.   Lon-
       don: Macdonald, 1961.   206p.

164.   KEETON, George Williams.   Trial for Treason.   Lon-
       don: Macdonald, 1959.   256p.

165.   KELLY, Tom.   Murders: Washington's Most Famous
       Murder Stories.   Washington, D. C. :   Washingtonian,
       1976.   129p.

166.   KELLY, Vincent.   The Charge Is Murder.   Adelaide:
       Rigby, 1965.   240p.

167.   KERSHAW, Alister.   Murder in France.   London: Con-
       stable, 1955.   188p.

168.   KETTLE, John, and Dean Walker.   Verdict!   Eleven
       Revealing Canadian Trials.   Toronto: McGraw-Hill,
       © 1968.   289p.

169. KHOSLA, Gopal Das. The Murder of the Mahatma, and
      Other Cases from a Judge's Note-Book. Foreword
      by the Right Honourable the Lord Evershed. London:
      Chatto & Windus, 1963. 245p.

170. KILGALLEN, Dorothy. Murder One. New York: Ran-
      dom House, 1967. 304p.

171. KING, Horace Maybray. State Crimes. London: Dent,
      1967. 162p.

172. KINGSTON, Charles. Society Sensations. London: Paul,
      1922. 253p.

173. KNOWLES, Leonard. Court of Drama. London: Long,
      1966. 176p.

174. KNOX, Bill. Court of Murder: Famous Trials at
      Glasgow High Court. London: Long, 1968. 192p.

175. KRAMER, Charles. The Negligent Doctor; Medical
      Malpractice in and Out of Hospitals and What Can Be
      Done About It. New York: Crown, 1968. 255p.

176. KUNSTLER, William Moses. ... And Justice for All.
      Dobbs Ferry, N.Y.: Oceana, 1963. 239p.

177. KUNSTLER, William Moses. The Case for Courage.
      New York: Morrow, 1962. 413p.

178. KUNSTLER, William Moses. First Degree. New York:
      Oceana, 1960. 239p.

179. LAMBERT, Richard S. When Justice Faltered; A Study
      of Nine Murder Trials. London: Methuen, 1935.
      283p.

180. LAMBTON, Arthur. Echoes of Causes Célèbres. Lon-
      don: Hurst & Blackett, 1931. 277p.

181. LAWSON, John Davidson, ed. American State Trials;
      A Collection of the Important and Interesting Crimi-
      nal Trials Which Have Taken Place in the United
      States, from the Beginning of Our Government to the
      Present Day. Notes and Annotations by John D. Law-
      son. St. Louis: Thomas Law Book, 1914-36. 17v.

182. LEVIN, David, ed. What Happened in Salem? Docu-
      ments Pertaining to the Seventeenth-Century Witch-
      craft Trials. Young Goodman Brown, by Nathaniel
      Hawthorne and A Mirror for Witches, by Esther Forbes.
      Second Edition. New York: Harcourt, Brace, 1960.
      238p.

183. LOGAN, Guy B. H. Dramas of the Dock. London:
      Paul, 1930. 286p.

184. LOGAN, Guy B. H. Great Murder Mysteries. London:
      Paul, 1931. 288p.

185. LOGAN, Guy B. H. Guilty or Not Guilty? London:
      Paul, 1928. 288p.

186. LOGAN, Guy B. H. Verdict and Sentence. London:
      Eldon, 1935. 280p.

187. LOGAN, Guy B. H. Wilful Murder. London: Eldon,
      1935. 280p.

188. LUCAS, Netley. Lord Darling and His Famous Trials;
      An Authentic Biography. Prepared (For Publication)
      Under the Personal Supervision of Lord Darling, by
      Evelyn Graham (pseud.) London: Hutchinson, 1929.
      287p.

189. LUSTGARTEN, Edgar. The Business of Murder. New
      York: Scribner, 1968. 218p.

190. LUSTGARTEN, Edgar Marcus. Defender's Triumph.
      Introduction by James Nelson. New York: Norton,
      1968. 238p.

191. LUSTGARTEN, Edgar. The Murder and the Trial.
      Edited and with an Introduction by Anthony Boucher.
      New York: Scribner, 1958. 340p.

192. LUSTGARTEN, Edgar. Verdict in Dispute. An Analysis
      of Six Famous Murder Trials. London: Wingate,
      1949. 253p.

193. LUSTGARTEN, Edgar Marcus. The Woman in the Case.
      New York: Scribner, 1955, 218p.

194. MACDONELL, Sir John. Historical Trials. Oxford:
      Clarendon, 1927. 234p.

195. MACKENZIE, Frederick Arthur. Twentieth Century
      Crimes. Illustrated from photographs. Boston: Little,
      Brown, 1927. 273p.
      Also published in London under title: World Famous
      Crimes.

196. MAKRIS, John N. , ed. Boston Murders, by Marjorie
      Carleton, and Others. New York: Duell, Sloan and
      Pearce, 1947. 223p. (Regional Murder Series, v. 9.)

197. MARSDEN, Philip Kitson. In Peril Before Parliament.
      Preface by Anthony Wedgwood Benn. New York: Roy,
      1966, © 1965. 270p.

198. McCLURE, James. Killers. London: Fontana, 1976.
      189p.

199. McCONNELL, Jean. The Detectives: Turning Points
      in Criminal Investigation. North Pomfret, Vt. : David
      and Charles, 1976. 160p.

200. McKOWN, Robin. Seven Famous Trials in History.
      Illustrated by William Sharp. New York: Vanguard,
      © 1963. 308p.

201. MEHTA, Hans Raj. Famous Indian Cases. Chandigarh:
      Kailash Law Publishers, 1964. 97p.

      MENZIES, Gordon, ed. see HISTORY Is My Witness

202. MIDDLEMISS, Herbert Samuel, ed. Hoodwinked Justice.
      Washington, D. C. : American Research Council, 1925.
      105p.

203. MOISEWITSCH, Maurice. Five Famous Trials. Com-
      mentaries by Lord Birkett. Greenwich, Conn. : New
      York Graphic Society, 1962. 209p.

204. MOISEWITSCH, Maurice. Four Famous Trials. Lon-
      don: Transworld, 1963. 158p.

205. MONGAN, James. A Report of Trials Before the Right
      Hon. the Lord Chief Justice, and the Hon. Baron Sir

Wm. C. Smith, Bart., at the Special Commission, at Maryborough, Commencing on the 23rd May, and Ending on the 6th June. Dublin: Milliken, 1832. 326p.

206.   MORLAND, Nigel. Background to Murder. London: Laurie, 1955. 224p.

207.   MORLAND, Nigel. Hangman's Clutch. London: Laurie, 1954. 239p.

208.   MORRIS, Richard Brandon. Fair Trial; Fourteen Who Stood Accused, from Anne Hutchinson to Alger Hiss. Revised Edition. New York: Harper & Row, 1967. 494p.

209.   MORSE, John T. Famous Trials. Boston: Little, Brown, 1874. 342p.

210.   MURIEL, John St. Clair. Doctors of Murder. London: Long, 1962. 176p.

211.   MYSTERIES of Crime, As Shown in Remarkable Capital Trials, by a Member of the Massachusetts Bar. Boston: Walker, 1870, © 1869. 431p.
       Also published under title: Celebrated Murders....

212.   NIZER, Louis. The Jury Returns. Garden City, N.Y.: Doubleday, 1966. 438p.

213.   NIZER, Louis. My Life in Court. Garden City, N.Y.: Doubleday, 1961. 542p.

214.   NOORANI, Abdul Gafoor Abdul Majeed. Indian Political Trials. New Delhi: Sterling, 1976. 259p.

215.   O'BRIEN, Frank Michael. Murder Mysteries of New York. New York: Payson, 1932. 231p.

216.   O'DONNELL, Bernard. Trials of Mr. Justice Avory. London: Rich & Cowan, 1935. 280p.

217.   O'DONNELL, Bernard. The World's Strangest Murders. London: Muller, 1957. 228p.

218.   PAGET, Reginald Thomas, and S. S. Silverman. Hanged

--and Innocent? Epilogue by Christopher Hollis.
London: Gollancz, 1953. 278p.

219. PARMITER, Geoffrey de Clinton. Reasonable Doubt.
London: Barker, 1938. 331p.

220. PARRIS, John. Most of My Murders. London: Muller, 1960. 288p.

221. PARRY, Leonard Arthur. Some Famous Medical Trials.
Introduction by Willard Huntington Wright. Fairfield,
N. J.: Kelly, 1976. 326p.
Reprint of 1928 edition published by Scribner, New York.

222. PASLEY, Fred D. Not Guilty! The Story of Sam Lei-
bowitz. New York: Putnam, 1933. 281p.

223. PEARSON, Edmund. Five Murders; With a Final Note
on the Borden Case. Garden City, N. Y.: Published
for the Crime Club, by Doubleday, Doran, 1928. 294p.

224. PEARSON, Edmund Lester. Murder at Smutty Nose
and Other Murders. London: Heinemann, 1927. 330p.

225. PEARSON, Edmund Lester. Studies in Murder. New
York: Macmillan, 1924. 295p.

226. PHILLIPS, Conrad. Murderer's Moon: Being Studies
of Heath, Haigh, Christie & Chesney. London: Barker, 1956. 238p.

227. PLAYFAIR, Giles, and Derrick Sington. The Offen-
ders; the Case Against Legal Vengeance. New York:
Simon and Schuster, 1957. 305p.

228. PLAYFAIR, Giles. Six Studies in Hypocrisy. London:
Secker & Warburg, 1969. 248p.

229. POSTGATE, Raymond. Murder, Piracy and Treason;
A Selection of Notable English Trials. New York:
Houghton Mifflin, 1925. 254p.

230. POYNTER, James William. Forgotten Crimes. New
York: Macauley, 1930. 285p.

231. RADIN, Edward D. Crimes of Passion. New York:
Putnam, 1953. 247p.

232. RANDALL, Leslie. The Famous Cases of Sir Bernard
      Spilsbury. London: Nicholson and Watson, 1936.
      319p.

233. REYNOLDS, Quentin James. Courtroom; The Story of
      Samuel S. Leibowitz. Freeport, N. Y.: Books for
      Libraries, 1970, © 1950. 419p.

234. RICE, Craig, ed. Los Angeles Murders. New York:
      Duell, Sloan and Pearce, 1947. 249p.

235. ROBERTS, Carl Eric Bechhofer. The New World of
      Crime: Famous American Trials. Introductory Es-
      say on the Reading of Criminal Trials by Roland Bur-
      rows. London: Eyre and Spottiswoode, 1933. 241p.
      Also published under title: Famous American Trials.

236. ROSENBLATT, Stanley M. Malpractice and Other Mal-
      feasances. Secaucus, N. J.: Lyle Stuart, 1977. 352p.

237. ROSENTHAL, Eric. Apology Refused. London: Bailey
      Bros. & Swinfen, 1959. 187p.

238. ROUGHEAD, William. The Art of Murder. Foreword
      by Joseph Henry Jackson. New York: Sheridan
      House, 1943. 309p.

239. ROUGHEAD, William. Classic Crimes; A Selection
      from the Works of William Roughead. New York:
      Vintage, 1977. 449p.
      Reprint of 1951 edition published by Cassell, London.

240. ROUGHEAD, William. The Evil That Men Do. Com-
      piled with an Introduction by Edmund Pearson. Gar-
      den City, N. Y.: Published for the Crime Club, by
      Doubleday, Doran, 1929. 2v.

241. ROUGHEAD, William. Famous Crimes. London: Fa-
      ber and Faber, 1943. 318p.

242. ROUGHEAD, William. The Fatal Countess and Other
      Studies. Edinburgh: Green, 1924. 298p.

243. ROUGHEAD, William. Glengarry's Way, and Other
      Studies. Edinburgh: Green, 1922. 307p.

244. ROUGHEAD, William. Knave's Looking-Glass. London:
      Cassell, 1935. 325p.

245. ROUGHEAD, William. Neck or Nothing. London: Cassell, 1939. 277p.

246. ROUGHEAD, William. Rascals Revived. London: Cassell, 1940. 332p.

247. ROUGHEAD, William. The Riddle of the Ruthvens and Other Studies. Edinburgh: Green, 1919. 544p.

248. ROUGHEAD, William. Tales of the Criminous; A Selection from the Works of William Roughead, Together with Fourteen Letters to the Author from Henry James. London: Cassell, 1956. 266p.

249. ROUGHEAD, William. 12 Scots Trials. London: Green, 1913. 302p.

250. ROUGHEAD, William. What Is Your Verdict? London: Faber & Faber, 1931. 318p.

251. ROWAN, David. Famous American Crimes. London: Muller, 1957. 204p.

252. ROWAN, David. Famous European Crimes. London: Muller, 1955. 190p.

253. ROWLAND, John. Criminal Files. London: Arco, 1957. 178p.

254. ROWLAND, John. More Criminal Files. London: Arco, 1958. 158p.

255. ROWLAND, John. Poisoner in the Dock: Twelve Studies in Poisoning. London: Arco, 1960. 239p.

256. ROWLAND, John. Unfit to Plead? Four Studies in Criminal Responsibility. London: Long, 1965. 192p.

257. RUBENSTEIN, Richard E., comp. Great Courtroom Battles. Chicago: Playboy Press; distributed by Simon & Schuster, 1973. 305p.

258. RUNYON, Damon. Trials and Other Tribulations. Philadelphia: Lippincott, 1947. 285p.

259. RUSSELL, Donn, ed. Best Murder Cases. London: Faber and Faber, 1958. 272p.

260. RUSSELL, Edward Frederick Langley Russell (Baron).
      Though the Heavens Fall. London: Cassell, 1956.
      250p.

261. SANDERSON, Edgar. Judicial Crimes. A Record of
      Some Famous Trials in English History. London:
      Hutchinson, 1902. 263p.

262. SARKAR, Subodh Chandra. Notable Indian Trials. Sec-
      ond Edition. Calcutta: Sarkar, 1948. 246p.

263. SCHMALZBACH, Oscar R. Profiles in Murder. Lon-
      don, Sydney: Hodder and Stoughton, 1971, © 1971.
      161p.

264. SCHOFIELD, William Greenough. Treason Trail. Chi-
      cago: Rand McNally, 1964. 266p.

265. SEAGLE, William. Acquitted of Murder. Chicago:
      Regnery, 1958. 257p.

266. SEARCH, Marion Pamela, ed. Great True Crime Sto-
      ries. London: Arco, 1957. 2v.

267. SEIGENTHALER, John. A Search for Justice. Nash-
      ville: Aurora, 1971. 416p.

268. SELLERS, Alvin Victor. Classics of the Bar; Stories
      of the World's Great Legal Trials and a Compilation
      of Forensic Masterpieces. Washington, D.C.: Wash-
      ington Law Book, 1942. 8v.

269. SHERESKY, Norman. On Trial: Masters of the Court-
      room. New York: Viking, 1977. 246p.

270. SHRIVER, George H., ed. American Religious Here-
      tics; Formal and Informal Trials. Nashville: Abing-
      don, 1966. 240p.

      SIMPSON, Helen, et al. see The ANATOMY of Mur-
      der

271. SIX Trials. Robert S. Brumbaugh, ed. New York:
      Crowell, 1969. 126p.

272. SMITH, Edward Henry. Famous American Poison Mys-
      teries. London: Hurst & Blackett, 1926. 286p.

273. SMITH-HUGHES, Jack. Eight Studies in Justice. Lon-
      don: Cassell, 1953. 228p.

274. SMITH-HUGHES, Jack. Nine Verdicts on Violence.
      London: Cassell, 1956. 219p.

275. SMITH-HUGHES, Jack. Six Ventures in Villainy. Lon-
      don: Cassell, 1955. 227p.

276. SMITH-HUGHES, Jack. Unfair Comment upon Some
      Victorian Murder Trials. London: Cassell, 1951. 360p.

277. SPAIN, David M. Post Mortem. Garden City, N. Y. :
      Doubleday, © 1974. 296p.

278. SPARROW, Gerald. Murder Parade. London: Hale,
      1957. 190p.

279. SPICER, Henry. Judicial Dramas; or, The Romance
      of French Criminal Law. London: Tinsley, 1872. 423p.

280. STEPHEN, Sir Harry Lushington, ed. State Trials; Poli-
      tical and Social. London: Duckworth, 1899-1902.
      New York: Kraus, 1971. 4v. in 2 (v. 3-4: Second
      Series).

281. STORIES of Great Crimes & Trials, from American Herit-
      age Magazine. Introduction by Oliver Jensen. New
      York: American Heritage; distributed by McGraw-
      Hill, 1974, © 1973. 382p.

282. SYMONS, Julian. A Reasonable Doubt; Some Criminal
      Cases Re-examined. London: Cresset, 1960. 223p.

283. TALLANT, Robert. Ready to Hang. New York: Har-
      per, 1952. 241p.
      Also published under title: Murder in New Orleans:
      Seven Famous Trials.

284. THOMAS, Donald, ed. State Trials. London: Routledge
      and Kegan Paul, 1972. 2v.
      v. 1: Treason and Libel
      v. 2: The Public Conscience

285. THOMPSON, Charles John Samuel. Poisons and Poison-
      ers, with Historical Accounts of Some Famous Mys-

teries in Ancient and Modern Times. London: Shaylor, 1931. 392p.

286. TOWNSEND, William Charles, ed. Modern State Trials.
      Revised and Illustrated with Essays and Notes. London: Longman, Brown, Green, and Longmans, 1850.
      2v.

287. TRACY, John Evarts. Nine Famous Trials. New York:
      Vantage, 1960. 176p.

288. TRAINI, Robert. Murder for Sex, and Cases of Manslaughter Under the New Act. London: Kimber, 1960.
      267p.

289. TREADWELL, Charles Archibald Lawrance. Notable
      New Zealand Trials. New Plymouth, N. Z. : Avery,
      1936. 314p.

290. TRIALS of the Resistance. Essays by Noam Chomsky,
      and Others, with an Introduction by Murray Kempton.
      New York: New York Review; distributed by Vintage,
      1970. 246p.

291. ULMAN, Joseph Nathan. A Judge Takes the Stand.
      New York: Knopf, 1933. 289p.

292. USHER, Frank Hugh. World Famous Acquittals, by Charles
      Franklin. (pseud.) Feltham: Odhams, 1970. 272p.

293. USHER, Frank Hugh. World Famous Trials: The Conflict and Drama of History's Greatest Court-Room
      Classics, by Charles Franklin. (pseud.) London:
      Odhams, 1966. 320p.

294. USHER, Frank Hugh. The World's Worst Murderers;
      Exciting and Authentic Accounts of the Great Classics
      of Murder, by Charles Franklin. (pseud.) London:
      Odhams, 1965. 320p.

295. VAN WINKLE, Marshall. Sixty Famous Cases: 29
      English Cases--31 American Cases, from 1778 to the
      Present. Long Branch, N. J. : Ayres, 1956. 10v.

296. WALBROOK, Henry Mackinnon. Murders and Murder
      Trials. London: Constable, 1932. 366p.

297. WALKER-SMITH, Derek. Lord Reading and His Cases;
      The Study of a Great Career. New York: Macmillan,
      1934. 400p.

298. WALLACE, William Stewart. Murders and Mysteries;
      A Canadian Series. Toronto: Macmillan, 1931.
      333p.

299. WEBLEY, Laurence. Across the Atlantic. London:
      Stevens, 1960. 331p.

300. WEST, Luther C. They Call It Justice; Command In-
      fluence and the Court-Martial System. New York:
      Viking, 1977. 302p.

301. WEST, Rebecca (pseud.). Train of Powder. New York:
      Viking, 1955. 310p.

302. WHARTON, Francis. State Trials of the United States
      During the Administrations of Washington and Adams,
      with References, Historical and Professional, and
      Preliminary Notes on the Politics of the Times. New
      York: Franklin, 1970. 727p.

303. WHITTINGHAM, Richard. Famous Criminal Trials, by
      Andrew David (pseud.). Minneapolis: Lerner, 1979.
      128p. (On Trial Series.)

304. WHITTINGHAM, Richard. Famous Military Trials, by
      Andrew David (pseud.). Minneapolis: Lerner, 1980.
      120p. (On Trial Series.)

305. WHITTINGHAM, Richard. Famous Political Trials, by
      Andrew David (pseud.). Introduction by Dan Cohen.
      Minneapolis: Lerner, 1980. 112p. (On Trial Series.)

306. WHITTINGHAM, Richard. Famous Supreme Court
      Trials, by Andrew David (pseud.). Minneapolis:
      Lerner, 1980. 120p. (On Trial Series.)

307. WILD, Roland. Crimes and Cases of 1933-34. Lon-
      don: Rich & Cowan, 1934-35. 2v.

308. WILLIAMS, Bond. Due Process; The Fabulous Story
      of Criminal Lawyer George T. Davis and His Thirty-
      Year Battle Against Capital Punishment. New York:
      Morrow, 1960. 336p.

309. WILLIAMSON, William Henry. Annals of Crime; Some
      Extraordinary Women. London: Routledge, 1930.
      285p.

310. WILLIS-BUND, John William Bend. A Selection of
      Cases from the State Trials. Trials for Treason.
      Edited for the Syndics of the University Press. Cam-
      bridge, Eng.: University Press, 1879-82. 2v. in 3.

311. WILSON, John Gray. Not Proven. London: Secker &
      Warburg, 1960. 255p.

312. WORTH, Anthony. Consider Your Verdict. London:
      Yates, 1949. 127p.

313. WRIGHT, Sewell Peaslee, ed. Chicago Murders, by
      Elizabeth Bullock, and Others. New York: Duell,
      Sloan and Pearce, 1945. 213p. (Regional Murder
      Series, v. 2.)

314. WYNDHAM, Horace. Blotted 'Scutcheons; Some Society
      Causes Célèbres. Illustrated. London: Hutchinson,
      1926. 288p.

315. WYNDHAM, Horace. Consider Your Verdict. London:
      Allen, 1946. 207p.

316. WYNDHAM, Horace. Dramas of the Law. Illustrated.
      London: Hutchinson, 1936. 293p.

317. WYNDHAM, Horace. Famous Trials Re-told; Some So-
      ciety Causes Célèbres. London: Hutchinson, 1925.
      255p.

318. WYNDHAM, Horace. Judicial Dramas; Some Society
      Causes Célèbres. London: Unwin, 1927. 322p.
      Also published under title: Crimes in High Life;
      Some Society Causes Célèbres.

319. WYNDHAM, Horace. The Mayfair Calendar; Some So-
      ciety Causes Célèbres. London: Hutchinson, 1925.
      288p.

320. WYNDHAM, Horace. Society Sensations. London: Hale,
      1938. 282p.

321. WYNDHAM, Horace. Victorian Parade. London: Mul-
      ler, 1934. 304p.

322. WYNDHAM, Horace. Victorian Sensations. London:
      Jarrolds, 1933. 288p.

Sources Cited

Abbott, Burton W.	41, 79, 308
Abbott, William Henry	166
Abdullah, Sheikh Mohammed	214
Abel, Rudolf Ivanovich	150
Abrahams	128
Abrams, Jacob, et al.	268v. 6
Acid-Bath Murderer <u>see</u> Haigh, John George	
Adams, Francis	205
Adams, John Bodkin (Dr.)	101v. 4, 161
Adams, Paul (Sgt.)	300
Adams, Richard	
Adams v. Miami-Dade County Jail	236
Adams, Seth	
Millspaugh v. Adams	68
Adamson, John Michael	21
African Ballet	168
Afro-American (Newspaper) Co.	
Macrea v. Afro-American Co.	91
Aga Khan: Begum Aga Khan Jewel Robbery	252
Agate, James	
Agate v. Guardian Publications Ltd.	15
Agostini, Antonio	66
Ahmed, Khwaja Nazir	103
Ahmed, Shafi, et al.	4, 105, 262
Aiyangar, Ramanujam	4
Alabama Arbitration	133
Alex, Michael	265
Alexander, Alexander (claimed Earl of Stirling)	286v. 1
Algarron, Jacques	109

*Includes plaintiffs for civil cases.

31

Ali, Maulana Mohammed & Maulana
    Shaukat   214
Allaway, Thomas Henry   110, 147, 216, 312
Allcard, Mary
    Allcard v. Skinner   315
Allen
    Allen v. Flood   297
Allen, Daniel K.   181v. 12
Allen, Frances Caroline
    Allen v. Frayne   162
Allen, Margaret   146
Allen, William Philip, et al.   43
Alley, John, Jr.   181v. 14
Allison, Henry B., et al.   181v. 4
Alvaro, George
    Alvaro v. Washington Hospital
    (NYC) & Dr. Rhenston   175
Amalgamated Woodworkers' Interna-
    tional Union   268v. 4
Ambrister, Robert C.   181v. 2
American Medical Association
    Chattanooga Medicine Co. v. Ameri-
    can Medical Association   295v. 4
American Mercury (Boston)   130
Amistad (Schooner)   98, 287
Ancarola, Antonio   181v. 3
Anderson, John: John Anderson
    Will Case   295v. 4
André, John (Maj.)   44v. 2, 62v. 2, 181v. 6,
                                             235

Andrea Doria/Stockholm
    Ricolo v. Andrea Doria/
    Stockholm   9
Anglesea (Lord)
    Annesly v. Lord Anglesea   51, 129, 280v. 4, 287
Annesly, James
    Annesly v. Lord Anglesea   51, 129, 280v. 4, 287
Anstruther, Sir Alexander   243
Anthony, Susan B.   181v. 3, 295v. 10
Antoinette, Marie see Marie An-
    toinette
Antonini, Joseph, et al.   95
Applegate, Everett C.   170
Apte, Narayan D., et al.   75
Aram, Eugene   33, 36, 52, 123, 148
Arbuckle, Roscoe "Fatty"   231, 268v. 8
Arbuthnot, Alexander   181v. 2

Archer-Gilligan (Mrs.)   272
Archer-Shee, George   46, 111
Arden, Alice, et al.   34
Ardlamont Mystery see Monson,
    Alfred John
Armstrong, Herbert Rouse (Maj.)   17, 47, 113, 137, 148,
                                               187, 188, 232, 259,
                                               285, 312
Armstrong, John & Janet   101v. 4
Armstrong, William "Duff"   2, 208
Army-McCarthy Hearings   177
Arnold, Benedict (Maj. Gen.)   84, 181v. 6, 235
Arnold, Samuel   181v. 8
Arnold the Miller
    Arnold the Miller v. Baron von
        Gersdorf   287
Arran Murder see Laurie, John
    Watson
Arrison, William   181v. 5
Atzerodt, George A.   181v. 8
Auchindrayne: Lord of Auchindrayne
        see Murc, John (Lord of
        Auchindrayne)
Austin, Charles
    Austin v. Disraeli   65
Avery, Edward T.   181v. 9
Avery, Ephraim K. (Rev.)   211, 224
Avril, Robert   101v. 5
Axis Sally see Gillars, Mildred
Ayalik, Jimmy   168
Ayliffe, John   93
Azad, Maulana Abul Kalam   214
Azad, Singh   295v. 8

Baby Lenore Case see De Martino,
    Nick & Jean
Baccarat Scandal see Wilson,
    Arthur Stanley, et al.
Bacon, Francis   37
Badham, George Alexander   15
Baffier, Jean   18
Bagg, Arthur Richard   29
Bailey, Francis Lee   13
Bailey, Raymond John   66, 166
Bailey, William (Rev.)   317

Baillet   18
Baillie, Thomas (Capt.)
    Board of Admiralty v. Baillie   92v. 1
Baillie-Stewart, Norman (Lt.):
        1933 Trial   307v. 1
        1945 Trial   38
Bainbrigge, Betty
    Thomas Parker Bainbrigge v.
        Betty Bainbrigge   172, 230
Baker, Valentine (Col.)   228, 317, 322
Baker Estate Swindle see Smith,
        Cameron, et al.
Bakke, Allan
    Regents of the University of Cali-
        fornia v. Bakke   306
Balham Mystery see Cox, Jane
        Cannon
Ball, Edward   77
Ball, George   78
Ball, John   181v. 7
Ball, Lee   202
Ballem, Francis Xavier   79
Ballew, Stephen M.   181v. 7
Baltimore: Lord Baltimore see
        Calvert, Frederick (Baron of
        Baltimore)
Banbury: Earldom of Banbury
    Knollys v. Earldom of Banbury   92v. 4
Banerjee, Surendranath
    Banerjee v. Norris   104, 262
Bangor: Bishop of Bangor, et al.   92v. 4
Banks, Harold Chamberlain   168
Barber, William Henry   8, 70
Baring, Rupert (Lord Revelstoke)
    Joyce v. Baring   15
Barlow, Kenneth   101v. 5, 255
Barlow, Silas   49
Barnard, William   51, 280v. 4
Barnes, Peter, et al.   141
Barnes, William, Jr.
    Barnes v. Roosevelt   295v. 7
Barneveldt, Jan van Olden   261
Barney, Elvira Dolores   128, 148, 190, 191, 228,
                                                253, 259

Baron, Maurice
    Baron v. Leo Feist, Inc.   213

Barron, James (Commo.)   84
Bartlett, Adelaide   7, 108, 120, 123, 135,
                                          149, 180, 190, 191,
                                          203, 206, 238, 241,
                                          250, 255, 292, 296

Bastide, Louis, et al.   120
Bastien   34, 279
Bastwick, John (Dr.)   284v. 1
Bateman, Charles (Dr.)   221
Bateman, Mary   33, 148
Bauer, Gustav   117
Bawla--Abdul Bawla Murder   see
     Ahmed, Shafi, et al.
Baxter, Richard   229, 284v. 1
Bayard, Nicholas (Col.)   37, 62v. 1, 181v. 10
Bayly, William Alfred   7, 254
Beall, John Y.   181v. 14
Beamish, Richard Piggott
     Pike v. Beamish   45
Beauchamp, Jeroboam O.   160
Beauvallon, Rosamond de   121
Beck, Adolf   42, 46, 148, 154, 216,
                                          219
Beck, Martha   110, 251
Becker, Charles (Lt.)   178, 195
Becker, Max   222
Beecher, Henry Ward (Rev.)
     Tilton v. Beecher   11, 268v. 1
Been, Hyman
     Been v. Sears, Roebuck & Co.   236
Belaney, Archivald Stansfield see
     Grey Owl Estate Suit
Bell, James L.   181v. 14
Bell, Jared W.   181v. 3
Bellingham, John   33, 44v. 2, 48v. 2, 148,
                                          296, 299
Belt, Richard Claude
     Belt v. Lawes   125, 314
Bembridge, Charles   92v. 2
Bennett, George   127
Bennett, Herbert John   157, 184, 207, 282
Benoit, Frédéric   118
Benson, Harry   17, 199
Bentley, Derek William   101v. 1, 111, 115, 157,
                                          218, 220
Benton, Wallace   147

Berger, Bertha   308
Berger, Ralph   306
Berkeley, Frederick Augustus (5th
        Earl of Berkeley)   48v. 1
Berland, Adolphe, et al.   18
Bernardy de Sigoyer   167
Berrange, James Louis Steyn
    Berrange v. Mavrogordato   237
Berrigan, Philip see Harrisburg 7
Bertrand, Henry Louis   7, 97v. 1, 156
Besant, Annie   104
Besnard, Marie   252, 292
Best, Robert   264
Beswick, Frederick (Maj.)   317
Better Business Bureau of Greater
        Philadelphia
    Volunteers of America v. Better
        Business Bureau of Greater
        Philadelphia   91
Bhattacharjee, Taranath (Dr.)   4
Bhowal Sannyasi Case   75, 262
Bichel, Andrew   95
Biggs, Ronald Arthur, et al.   111
Billik, Herman   272
Billings, Warren   131
Bingham, Richard
    Howard v. Bingham   92v. 4
Birch, Leroy, et al. see Dragon
        Gang (N. Y.)
Birchall, John Reginald   184, 298
Bird, Thomas   181v. 14
Bishop, Bridget   181v. 1, 182
Bishop, John   273
Bjorkland, Diane   79
Black, Crawford   165, 268v. 1-2
Black Panthers (Chicago)   39
Blackburn, Joseph   93
Blair, John   54
Blake (Lt.)
    Blake v. Wilkins   43
Blake, Patrick   181v. 1
Blanck, Max see Triangle Fire
        Case
Blandford: Marquis of Blandford
    Marquis of Blandford v. The
        Satirist (Journal)   172

Blandy, Mary   40, 123, 135, 248, 319
Blood, Thomas (Col.)   36, 148, 318
Blount, William (Sen.)   302
Blyth, Irene Adelaide   23
Board of Admiralty
  Board of Admiralty v. Baillie   92v. 1
Board of Union Free School District
      No. 9, New Hyde Park (N.Y.)
  Engel v. Board of Union Free
      School District No. 9   176
Boatman, Antoinette
  Boatman v. Osteopathic General
      Hospital, Miami   236
Bodine, Polly   68
Bogart, Abraham   181v. 5
Boggie, Clarence Gilmore   42
Bokhari, Attaullah Shah   103
Boland, Jack "Bobo"   165
Boleyn, Anne (Queen of Henry VIII
      of England)   87, 129, 310v. 1
Bolo Pascha   1
Bolton, Mildred   313
Bompard, Gabrielle   153, 207, 254
Bonaparte, Pierre Napoleon (Prince)   209
Bond Street Mystery see Leverson,
      Sarah Rachel
Bonds, Jack Whitfield   85
Bonnet, Stede "Major", et al.   181v. 4
Bonnie, Lola Ida Hemri   165
Boorn, Stephen & Jesse   120, 181v. 6, 211, 225
Booth, Handel   128
Boott, William   181v. 3
Borden, Lizzie   11, 161, 178, 186, 191,
                                          192, 223, 224, 225,
                                          257, 292, 294

Borgmann, Margaret
  Borgmann v. Hillary Hospital (NYC)
      & Dr. Wilson   175
Boston Five   14
Boston Massacre Soldiers   62v. 1, 98, 177, 281
Boston Strangler see DeSalvo, Albert
Botha, Louis (P. M. of South Africa)
  Botha v. Munnik   237
Botkin, Cordelia   155, 272
Bottomley, Horatio William   17, 111, 132, 148, 149,
                                          295v. 3

Bounty (Ship) Mutineers see Hey-
    wood, Peter, et al.
Bouvier, Léone   109
Bowen, George   181v. 1
Bower, Elliott   179, 320
Bowers, J. Milton (Dr.)   272
Bowes, Andrew Robinson   275
Bowne, Borden Parker   270
Boyer, Marie   153
Brace, Philander   181v. 15
Bradley, Stephen Leslie   166
Bradstreet, Martha   181v. 17
Bram, Thomas Mead Chambers   187, 225
Branch, Elizabeth & Betty   238, 245
Brancusi, Constantin
    Brancusi v. U. S. Customs   3
Brand, Elizabeth & Maria   30, 48v. 2
Brandreth, Jeremiah, et al.   48v. 2
Bravo, Florence   121, 180, 239, 241, 250
Bray, George James (Sgt.)   274
Breeds, John   273
Brekke, Carstein   207
Brennan, Ian   21
Breton (Major)   18
Brettinger, Rudi   227
Brides in the Bath Case see Smith,
    George Joseph
Brierly, John, et al.   181v. 4
Briggs, Charles Augustus   270
Bright Star Hospital (NYC), Dr.
    Lawrence, et al. :
    Mele v. Bright Star Hospital,
      Dr. Lawrence, et al.   175
Brighton Police Case   101v. 5
Brighton Trunk Murder see Mancini,
    Toni
Brinvilliers: Marquise de Brinvilliers
    see D'Aubray, Marie Mar-
    guerite (Marquise de Brinvil-
    liers)
Bristol: Countess of Bristol see
    Pierrepoint, Elizabeth (Duchess
    of Kingston)
British South Africa Co.   36
Brodie, Deacon   36, 148, 239, 244
Brooks, Gertrude
    Brooks v. Conston   91

Brooks, Hugh M.   181v. 13
Broughton, Sir Henry John Delves   282
Brown, Charles T.   60
Brown, Charles Templeman   174
Brown, E. M. (Dr.)   67
Brown, Ernest   307v. 1
Brown, Francis Wayland   54
Brown, J. B.   120
Brown, James   127, 298
Brown, John (Capt.)   89v. 2, 98, 133, 181v.
                                              6, 208, 235, 271, 281

Brown, John Whelan   66
Brown, Linda
  Brown v. Board of Education,
    Topeka, Kansas   306
Brown, Orville H.
  Brown v. Davidson   68
Browne, Frederick Guy   74, 128, 147, 148, 180,
                                              185, 199, 216, 312

Browning, Edward W.
  Frances "Peaches" Browning v.
    Edward Browning   258
Brudenell, James Thomas (Earl of
    Cardigan)   51, 65, 102, 148, 197,
                                              230, 286v. 1, 317,
                                              318

Bruneau, Albert (Abbé)   274
Bruno, Giordano   194
Bryan, Henry John, et al.   253
Bryant, Charlotte   61, 146, 255
Bryce, Mabel
  Francis Bryce v. Mabel Bryce
    & Pape   297
Buchalter, Louis "Lepke"   178
Buchanan, Robert
  Buchanan v. Taylor   316
Buchanan, Robert W. (Dr.)   215, 272
Buckhout, Isaac van Wart   67
Buckingham: Duke of Buckingham
    see Stafford, Edward (Duke
    of Buckingham)
Buckingham, Joseph T.   181v. 14
Buffum, Jonathan   181v. 14
Buford, Thomas (Col.)   160
Bulawayo Chronicle
  Johnson v. Bulawayo Chronicle   237

Bunce, Johnny	20
Burch, Arthur	234
Burgel, Gus	
Burgel v. Red Wing Carriers	236
Burgess, Richard	289
Burke, Francis	181v. 4
Burke, Jerry	
Burke v. Dr. Kessler & Parkway	
General Hospital, Miami	236
Burke, Kenneth Kenwyn	32
Burke, William	8, 33, 37, 86, 123, 148,
	221, 239, 244, 296
Burks, Harold Finnon "Arkansas"	231
Burnett, Kenneth	21
Burnham, Josiah	181v. 8
Burnopfield Mystery <u>see</u> Cain, John	
Burns, Anthony	181v. 5
Burns, Florence	215
Burr, Aaron (Sen.)	133, 208, 281, 287
Burroughs, George	181v. 1, 182
Burrows, Albert Edward	147
Bursey, Charles	39
Burtlett, Mike	165
Burton, Henry	284v. 1
Bury St. Edmunds Witchcraft Trials	65, 229, 284v. 2
Butler, Edward	181v. 9
Butler, Frank	97v. 2
Butler, Henry Edmund	
Pierce Butler v. Henry Butler	172
Butler, Robert	153, 289
Büttner, Ernest	69
Byng, John (Adm.)	50, 293
Byrne, Patrick Joseph	101v. 6, 288
Byron, Kittie	17
Byron, William (Lord)	51, 78, 280v. 4
Bywaters, Frederick Edward Francis	37, 47, 74, 78, 83, 110,
	113, 119, 148, 149,
	207, 219, 232
Cadbury, William	
Cadbury v. Evening Standard	297
Cadden, Mary Annie "Mamie"	76
Caddick, Alfred	220
Caffee, William	80
Cagli, Augusto	
Cagli v. Cape Mercury (Newspaper)	237

Caillaux, Henriette   11, 117, 167, 292
Caillaux, Joseph   1
Caille, Isaac de see Mège, Pierre
Cain, Alfred E.   39, 64
Cain, John   179
Cairns, Arthur William (Viscount Gar-
    moyle)
  Finney v. Cairns   314
Calas, Jean   261
Calder, Sir Robert (Vice Adm.)   50
Caldwell, Oscar T.   181v. 1
Callender, James Thomas   133, 181v. 10, 302
Calley, William L. (Lt.)   84, 257, 300, 304
Calvert, Frederick (Baron of Balti-
    more)   275
Calvert, Louie   146
Camb, James   29, 61, 96, 149, 282,
                                                          312
Cameron, Cecil Aylmer & Ruby   315, 317
Campbell, Colin (Lady)
  Lord Campbell v. Lady Campbell   172, 319
Campbell, Mungo   51
Campion, Edmund   310v. 1
Campisciano, Ignazio & Maria, et al.   283
Canning, Elizabeth   65, 260
Cant, George   70
Canter, Ben, et al.   101v. 3
Cape Mercury (Newspaper)
  Cagli v. Cape Mercury   237
Capone, Al   55, 257, 258
The Captive (Drama)   130
Carawan, George W. (Rev.)   181v. 6, 268v. 6
Cardigan: Earl of Cardigan see
        Brudenell, James Thomas
        (Earl of Cardigan)
Carey, Jahleel Brendon (Capt.)   315
Caritativo, Bart   79
Carlile, Richard   59
Carnal, Henri   68
Carnan, Thomas   92v. 1
Caroline (Queen of George IV of Gt.
    Brit.)
  George IV v. Caroline   48v. 2, 129, 197, 292,
                                                          318
Carpenter (Dr.), et al.   269
Carr, Albert George   23

Carr, Robert (Earl of Somerset) &
    Frances (Countess of Somerset)   44v. 1,102, 242
Carraher, Patrick   142
Carrington (Lord)   315
Carroll, Earl   295v. 7
Carroll, James, et al.   127, 298
Carson, Robert "Sonny"   13
Carter, George   101v. 6
Carter, Kid   196
Cartouche, Dominique   99, 279
Cartwright, Albert   237
Caruso, Francesco   178
Casement, Sir Roger   17, 36, 87, 111, 148,
        164, 216, 260, 293,
        297

Casey, James P.   181v. 15
Cass, Elizabeth   46
Castaing, Edme (Dr.)   153
Castro, Thomas see Orton, Arthur
Catherine of Aragon (Queen of Henry
    VIII of England)   10, 194
Cato Street Conspiracy   33, 44v. 2, 48v. 2, 87,
        171, 229
Catonsville Nine   14
Cauvin, Louis   309
Cavell, Edith   10, 11
Cedeno, Simon   289
Central News Agency
    Naylor v. Central News Agency   237
Cero, Gongi   196
Chaffers, Alexander
    Twiss v. Chaffers   316, 317
Chalkpits Murder see   Ley, Thomas J.
Chamberlain, Arthur
    Chamberlain v. The Star (News-
        paper)   297
Chandler, Douglas   264
Chantrelle, Eugène Marie   108
Chaplin, Edward Royal   15
Chapman
    Chapman v. Jockey Club   128
Chapman, George   135
Chapman, Lucretia   35, 181v. 6, 211, 238
Charing Cross Trunk Murder   see
        Robinson, John
Charles I (King of England)   10, 11, 37, 44v. 1, 82,
        87, 129, 148, 171,

	197, 280v. 1, 293, 310v. 1
Charles, Henri	259
Charlesworth, Violet	17
Chase, Samuel (Judge)	181v. 11
Chattanooga Medicine Co.	
Chattanooga Medicine Co. v. American Medical Association	295v. 4
Chemis, Louis	289
Cherry, Noah, et al.	181v. 3
Chesney, Donald	101v. 1, 226
Chessman, Caryl	9, 150, 308
Chetwynd, Sir George	
Chetwynd v. Durham	297, 319
Chetwynd, William	314
Chevallier, Yvonne Rousseau	109, 252
Chicago May see Churchill, May Vivienne	
Chicago 7	10, 303
Chicago Tribune	
Ford v. Chicago Tribune	295v. 6
Chigango, et al.	81
Childers, Sherod, et al.	181v. 9
Childs, Nathaniel, Jr.	181v. 2
Christie, John Reginald Halliday	31, 79, 96, 101v. 1, 189, 218, 226, 278, 288, 294
Christofi, Styllou	101v. 2, 146, 266v. 2
Churchill, May Vivienne	17
The Churchman (Journal)	
Hess v. The Churchman	295v. 7
Clare, Philip	230
Clark, Henry (Dr.)	4, 105, 110, 262
Clark, Joseph Reginald Victor	217
Clark, Stephen Merrill	181v. 6
Clark, Violet	101v. 4
Clarke, Mary Ann	48v. 1
Clausen, William	295v. 1
Cleft Chin Murder see Jones, Elizabeth Marina & Hulten, Karl Gustav	
Clements, Charles	289
Clerk, Duncan	240v. 1, 249, 250
Cleveland Street Scandal see Parke, Ernest	
Clive, Robert (Lord)	299

Cloncurry: 2nd Baron of Cloncurry
    see Lawless, Valentine
    Browne (2nd Baron of Clon-
    curry)
Clough, Ebenezer   181v. 3
Cluverius, Thomas J.   181v. 17
Coats, George Errol   289
Cobbett, William:
    Plunkett v. Cobbett   48v. 1, 92v. 4
    Rex v. Cobbett   37
    Rush v. Cobbett   181v. 6, 295v. 5, 302
Coburn, Edward O.   181v. 16
Cochran, Tom   13
Cochrane, Thomas (Earl of Dun-
    donald), et al.   36, 48v. 2, 261, 286v. 2
Cochrane Johnstone, Andrew James   275
Cock, Henry   93
Codrington, Helen Jane
    Henry Codrington v. Helen Codring-
       ton & Anderson   318
Coetzee, Jacobus Hendrik   25, 29
Coffey, William N.   80
Cohen, Louis
    Robinson v. Cohen   237
Coke, Arundel   52, 274
Colborne, John (Capt.)
    Davis v. Colborne   318
Cole, George W.   268v. 2
Coleman, Ronald   157
Collet, Anthelme   99
Colley (Rev.)
    Colley v. Maskeleyne   295v. 4
Collins, James   289
Collins, W. Maunsell (Dr.)   221
Colson, David (Col.)   160
Colt, John C.   89v. 1, 181v. 1
Comer, Jack, et al.   101v. 3
Communist (Newspaper)
    Thomas v. Communist   17
Conforte, Joe   42
Coningsmark (Count), et al.   280v. 3
Conston, Harry
    Brooks v. Conston   91
Coo, Eva   170
Cook, James   186
Cook, John E.   181v. 6, 268v. 4

Cook, W. J.   181v. 10
Coolidge, Valorus P. (Dr.)   181v. 3, 211
Cooper, Daniel Richard   289
Cooper, Thomas   181v. 10, 302
Coough, Joel   181v. 1
Copeland, John Anthony   181v. 6
Coppoc, Edwin   181v. 6
Coppolino, Carl (Dr.)   12, 41
Cora, Charles   181v. 15
Corday, Charlotte   89v. 1, 293
Corder, William   33, 89v. 1, 148, 211,
                                              296

Corey-Price Case   196
Cork Card Case see Beamish,
    Richard Piggott
Corneilison, John J.   160
Cornock, Rosina Ann (Mrs.)   61
Cornwallis, Charles (Lord)   102
Cotton, Mary Ann   179
Coulter, William   66
Council of Madras   92v. 4
Coupar, Robert Martin   31
Cournou, Etienne, et al.   18
Courvoisier, François Benjamin   8, 51, 89v. 1, 187,
                                              286v. 1, 296

Covell, Arthur   42
Cowper, Spencer, et al.   36, 51, 123, 148, 280v. 2
Cox, Frederick William   29
Cox, Jane Cannon   121, 180, 239, 241, 250
Cox, Robert Albion
    Cox v. Kean   228, 319
Coyle, Richard   44v. 2
Craig, Christopher   101v. 1, 111, 115, 157,
                                              218, 220

Craig, Eric Roland   116
Cramer, Anthony   177
Crapsey, Algernon Sidney   270
Crary, George D.   67
Crawford, Annie   283
Crawford, Virginia Mary
    Donald Crawford v. Virginia Craw-
        ford & Charles Dilke   172, 295v. 9, 314
Cream, Thomas Neill (Dr.)   86, 118, 135, 140, 159,
                                              191, 210, 221, 296,
                                              298, 313

Creighton, Mary Frances   170

Crick, William Patrick   69
Crimmins, Alice   277
Crippen, Hawley Harvey (Dr.)   47, 74, 90, 94, 124, 136,
                                        143, 148, 207, 210,
                                        221, 232, 255, 266v.
                                        1, 285, 294, 296
Crittenden, Thomas   160
Crockett, Simeon L.   181v. 1
Croker, Richard   67, 268v. 6
Crosland, Newton
    Pook v. Crosland   276
Cross, Philip (Dr.)   88, 315
Crosswell, Harry   181v. 16, 281
Crouch, Harriet Amelia   15
Crowe, Pat   295v. 8
Crowinshield, Richard, Jr.   181v. 7
Crump, Paul   212
Cudahy Case see Crowe, Pat
Cumberland: Duke of Cumberland see
        Henry Frederick (Duke of Cum-
        berland)
Cuming, Samuel   302
Cumming, John
    De Ros v. Cumming   45, 317
Cunningham, Emma Augusta   67, 181v. 5, 224
Cunningham, Sawney   211
Curll, Edmund   284v. 1
Curtis, Winslow   35
Custer, George Armstrong (Maj. Gen.) 84
Cuthell, John   92v. 4
Cutter Laboratories
    Gottsdanker v. Phipps & Cutter
        Laboratories   9, 257
Cvek, George Joseph   231
Czolgosz, Leon F.   181v. 14

Dacey, Edwin   220
Dague, Walter Glenn   126
Daily Mirror Newspapers Ltd. :
    Liberace v. Daily Mirror News-
        papers Ltd.   152
    Rex v. Daily Mirror Newspapers
        Ltd.   115
Daily Telegraph
    Risk Allah v. Daily Telegraph   276

Daley, Michael   300
Dalrymple, Charles John, et al.   243, 246
Dalton, Benjamin F.
  Commonwealth of Massachusetts v.
    Dalton & Coburn   181v. 16
Dalton, Helen Maria
  Benjamin Dalton v. Helen Dalton   181v. 16, 268v. 5
Dalton, James   181v. 14
Damiens, Robert Francis   34
D'Anglade (M. & Mme.)   279
Daniels, Henry   21
Darnes, William P.   181v. 16
Darrow, Clarence   268v. 8
Dasch, George, et al.   149
Dass, Janki
  Dass v. Movie Times (Journal)   103, 106
D'Aubray, Marie Marguerite (Mar-
    quise de Brinvilliers)   37, 86, 180
Dauphin Imposters   99
Davidson, Charles M.
  Brown v. Davidson   68, 268v. 7
Davies, Kathleen   101v. 1
Davies, Michael John   101v. 1, 157
Davis, Angela   10
Davis, Phineas
  Davis v. Colborne   318
Davison, Alexander   48v. 1
Davitt, Michael, et al.   43
Davy, Flora see Newington, Hannah
Dawes, Sophie   120, 273
Day, Thomas
  John Day v. Thomas Day   73
Dayton, John   181v. 2
Dean, Cyrus B.   181v. 3
Dean, George   69, 156
Dearnley, Albert   216
Debbs, Eugene Victor:
    1895 Trial   177, 295v. 7
    1918 Trial   295v. 7
De Beer, Petrus Cornelius   29
De Bernardi, Alain   252
De Champignelles, Rogres de Lusignan
  De Douhault v. De Champignelles   99
De Clifford (Lord)   295v. 8
DeCoster, Ezekiel, et al.   181v. 12
De Douhault (Marchioness)
  De Douhault v. De Champignelles   99

Deeming, Frederick Bailey	27, 28, 86, 97v. 2, 184
De Graff, William	223
De Lacy, Patrick O'Brien	217
De La Mare, E. G. (Mrs.)	253
Delany, John	205
Delany, Thomas, et al.	205
De Leeuw, Huibrecht Jacob	24, 30
De Leon, Ricardo	39, 64
Delgove (Justice of the Peace)	18
Delorme, Adelard (Abbé)	298
Deluca, Walter (Dr.)	
Harriman v. Deluca	175
Deluzy-Desportes, Henriette	238
De Marigny, Alfred (Count)	42, 149, 282
DeMartino, Nick & Jean	
Scarpetta v. DeMartino	236
De Melker, Daisy Louisa	26, 30
DeMina, Carolino	181v. 6
De Molen, Roger (Count)	18
Demon, Henri	109
Dennistoun, Ian (Lt. Col.)	
Dorothy Dennistoun v. Ian Dennistoun	16
De Pietro, Joseph	54
De Ros, Henry William (Lord)	
De Ros v. Cumming	45, 317
Derues, Antoine François	153
De Salis, Jean Baptiste, et al.	279
DeSalvo, Albert	12
Deschamps, Etienne	283
Desha, Isaac B.	160
Despard, Edward Marcus (Col.)	48v. 1, 50
Devereux, Robert (2nd Earl of Essex)	164, 280v. 3, 310v. 1
De Vidil, Alfred (Baron) see Vidil,	
Alfred de (Baron)	
DeVito, Mary	
DeVito v. United Airlines Co. &	
Douglas Aircraft Co.	9
DeVolkstem (Journal)	
Patterson v. DeVolkstem	237
DeWolf, Orrin	181v. 10
Dhingra, Madar Lal	295v. 8
Diamond Syndicate	128
Dias, Gilbert	5v. 2
Diblanc, Marguerite	276
Dick, Evelyn	168
Dickman, John Alexander	41, 123, 185

Dilke, Sir Charles Wentworth
  Donald Crawford v. Virginia
    Crawford & Dilke   172, 295v. 9, 314
Dillon, Arthur
  Dillon v. Miami-Dade County   236
Disney, Daniel (Maj.)   298
Disraeli, Benjamin (P. M. of Gt. Brit.)
  Austin v. Disraeli   65
Dobbs, Hannah   180, 183
Dobkin, Harry   199
Dockery, John   265
Dodd, William (Dr.)   33, 36, 51, 65, 93, 148,
                              314
Doineau, Auguste (Capt.)   274
Dominici, Gaston   101v. 2, 114, 150, 252
Donald, Jeannie   41, 244, 248
Donellan, John (Capt.)   44v. 2, 51, 242
Donelon, John Joseph (Mrs.)
  Donelon v. Long Island Railroad   213
Donovan, George Thomas   173, 216
Dooley, Alvin   233, 259
Dorland, Albert   20
Dorosier, Job   81
Dorr, Thomas Wilson   181v. 2
Doudet, Margarite Flore Célestine   309
Dougal, Samuel Herbert   135, 148
Douglas, Alfred (Lord)   152, 295v. 5
Douglas, John Sholto (Marquess of
    Queensberry)
  Wilde v. Douglas   10, 11, 75, 129, 292,
                              295v. 5
Douglas, Margaret   181v. 7
Douglas, Neil   71v. 2
Douglas Aircraft Co.
  DeVito v. United Airlines Co. &
    Douglas Aircraft Co.   9
The Doukhobors   168
Dove, William   49
Dowdall, Michael   288
Dowell, Kerry Ronald   263
Dowling, James   205
Dragon Gang (N. Y.)   178
Drayne, Moses   52
Dreyfus, Alfred (Maj.)   10, 11, 38, 82, 111, 114,
                              148, 171, 200, 271,
                              293, 305
Druaux, Pauline   118

Druce, Herbert	216
Duane, William	181v. 7, 302
Dubisson, Pauline	109, 252
Duca, Peter	126
Dudley, Thomas (Capt.), et al.	148, 276
Duker, Herman W.	291
Dumollard, Martin & Marianne	34, 279
Dunbar, Reuben	268v. 1
Dunbar, Ronald Patrick	101v. 5
Duncan, Leslie Fraser	
Knowles v. Duncan	316
Dundas, Henry (1st Viscount Melville)	48v. 1
Dunecht Mystery <u>see</u> Soutar, Charles	
Dunlo, Belle (Lady)	
Viscount Dunlo v. Lady Dunlo &	
Wertheimer	320
Dunne, Patrick	205
Du Plessis, Andries Stephanus	25, 29
Du Plessis, Dirkie Cathrina	25, 29
Du Randt, Ian	22, 32
Durant, James W. (Col.) & Kathleen B.	252
Durham (Lord)	
Chetwynd v. Durham	297, 319
Durham Clergy	
Williams v. Durham Clergy	286v. 2
Durrant, Henry Theodore	181v. 15, 184, 268v. 1, 295v. 8
Dustbin Case <u>see</u> Dennistoun, Ian	
(Lt. Col.)	
Du Tilh, Arnauld	99, 279
Dutilleul	18
Du Toit, Maria	22
Du Toit, Petrus Hendrik	30
Duval	1
Duval, Clément	18
Duvall, William Potts	80
Duveen, Sir Joseph	
Hahn v. Duveen	3
Dyer	289
Easterby, George	92v. 4
Eastland (Ship) Investigation	299
Eaton, Gerald	181v. 5
Eberle, Frederick	181v. 12
Edalji, George	42, 70, 118

Edgerly, George   12, 257
Edinburgh University Students' Riot
    see Dalrymple, Charles John,
    et al.
Edmonds, Edmund   276
Edmunds, Christina   296, 309
Edward (Earl of Warwick & Holland)   129, 280v. 2
Edwards, Carmen
    Edwards v. Missouri-Kansas-Texas
        Railroad Co., et al.   9
Edwards, Robert Allen   170
Eichmann, Adolf   9, 10, 11, 257, 305
Eidinoff, Harold (Dr.)   85
Eldredge, Laurence H.
    Musmanno v. Eldredge   91
Elgin, Thomas Bruce (Earl of Elgin)
    Elgin v. Ferguson   172, 318
Ellenborough, Jane (Lady)
    Lord Ellenborough v. Lady Ellen-
        borough   318
Elliott, Moses Chapman   211
Elliott, Robert J.   20
Ellis, Havelock, et al.   59
Ellis, Ruth   101v. 3
Ellis, Walter Scott   21
Elltoft, Sam   78
Emerson, Irene
    Scott v. Emerson   181v. 13
Emmet, Robert   48v. 1, 200, 268v. 5
Emmett-Dunne, Frederick (Sgt.)   38, 101v. 3, 254
Emond, Robert   238
Empire Steamship Co., Inc.
    Empire Steamship Co., Inc. v.
        Threadneedle Insurance Co.   15
Engel, George, et al.   181v. 12
Engel, Steven I., et al.
    Engel v. Board of Union Free
        School District No. 9, New
        Hyde Park, N.Y.   176
Enright, Larry
    Enright v. Winston   175
Epes, William Dandridge   181v. 3
Eppwright, Joseph   289
Escobedo, Danny   306
Esposimina, Lino Amalia   35, 238
Essex: Earl of Essex see Devereux,
    Robert (2nd Earl of Essex)

Euston: Countess of Euston see Fitz-
    roy, Kate Walsh (Countess of
    Euston)
Euston: Earl of Euston see Fitzroy,
    Henry (Earl of Euston)
Evans, Timothy John   119, 218
Evening Standard (Newspaper):
    Cadbury v. Evening Standard   297
    Jonesco v. Evening Standard   15
Eyerman, Jacob   181v. 11
Eyraud, Michel   153, 187, 207, 254
Eyre, Edward John   317

Fagan, Lewis (Dr.)
    Powell v. Fagan   236
Fahmy, Marie Marguerite   113, 149, 161, 278
Fahy, William   54
Faiman, Charles C. (Dr.)   54
Fair, Laura D.   181v. 15, 155, 209, 265
Fall, Albert see Teapot Dome Cases
Fanny Hill (Novel):
    Hackensack, N. J. Trial   257
    Toronto, Ont. Trial   168
Fantle, Ernest   101v. 6
Farrar, Sir George
    Farrar v. Madeley   237
Farwell, Hartwell   80
Faulk, John Henry
    Faulk v. Hartnett, Vincent, &
        Aware, Inc.   212
Fauntleroy, Henry   40, 93
Favre, Theodore
    Favre v. Monvoisin   67, 268v. 5
Fawcett, John
    Markham v. Fawcett   92v. 4, 268v. 4
Fawkes, Guy, et al.   11, 87, 310v. 1
Fawkner, John Pascoe
    St. John v. Fawkner   156
Feilding, Robert "Beau"   51, 65, 280v. 3
Fenayrou, Marion & Gabrielle   153
Fenian Invaders   127
Fenning, Elizabeth   119, 123
Ferguson, Robert
    Elgin v. Ferguson   172, 318
Fergusson, Alan   317

Fernandez, Raymond   110, 251
Ferrer, Francisco   11
Ferrers: 4th Earl of Ferrers see
      Shirley, Laurence (4th Earl
      of Ferrers)
Ferrers: 9th Earl of Ferrers see
      Shirley, Washington Sewallis
      (9th Earl of Ferrers)
Feuchères, Sophie de see Dawes,
      Sophie
Fichardt Ltd.
   Fichardt Ltd. v. The Friend (News-
      paper)   237
Field, Frederick   282
Field, Herbert Charles   307v. 1
Field, Jack Alfred   113, 137, 173, 216
Fielden, Samuel, et al.   181v. 12
Fifth Monarchy Rebellion   310v. 2pt. 1
Finch, Bernard (Dr.)   6, 170
Finney, Emily May
   Finney v. Cairns   314
Fiorenza, John   231
Fischer, Adolph, et al.   181v. 12
Fisher, Hubert William   31
Fisher, William   289
Fitzroy, Sir Almeric   149
Fitzroy, Henry (Earl of Euston)
   Euston v. Parke   152
Fitzroy, Kate Walsh (Countess of
      Euston)
   Earl of Euston v. Countess of
      Euston   172, 314
Flanagan, Anna & Sarah   289
Fleming, John   76
Fletcher, Susan   320
Flood
   Allen v. Flood   297
Foerster, Friedrich
   Foerster v. Ridder   213
Fontana, John   181v. 12
Fook, Liu   155
Foote, George William, et al.   59
Forbes, James   48v. 2
Ford, Arthur Kendrich   255
Ford, Clara   298
Ford, Henry:

Ford v. Chicago Tribune	295v. 6
Sapiro v. Ford	295v. 6
Ford, Wayne	168
Forrest, Catherine	
Catherine Forrest v. Edwin Forrest	172
Forster, John Paul	95
Forster, Philip	52
Fort Hood Three	14
Fortescue (Miss) see Finney, Emily May	
Fowler, Henry	132, 180, 216
The Fox see Hickman, William Edward	
Fox, Sidney	47, 113, 138, 162, 173, 186, 198, 232, 312
Francasal Case	101v. 1
Frank, Leo M.	56, 131, 176, 181v. 10
Frankfort (Viscount)	319
Franz, Frank	97v. 1
Fraser, Colin	
Fraser v. Hertzog	237
Fraser, Simon (12th Baron Lovat)	164, 197
Frayne	
Allen v. Frayne	162
Frederick Augustus (Duke of York)	48v. 1
Freeman, William	177, 181v. 16, 268v. 3
Frémont, John Charles (Lt. Col.)	299
French, Thaddeus P.	181v. 2
The Friend (Newspaper)	
Fichardt Ltd. v. The Friend	237
Fries, John	181v. 11
Fries, John see also Northampton Insurgents	
Frisch, Casper	95, 211
Fritz, Ernest	144
Frost, John (1750-1842)	92v. 2
Frost, John (d. 1877)	229, 286v. 1
Frothingham, David	
Hamilton v. Frothingham	302
Fruehauf, Roy	212
Fry, J. S. & Sons, Ltd.	
Tolley v. Fry & Sons, Ltd.	15
Fuchs, Claus	111
Fulham, Agatha	4, 105, 110, 262

Gaekwar, Mulhar Rao   214
Gaiety Girl Divorce Case see Bryce,
    Mabel
Gale, Sarah   33, 183
Galentine, Jay F. (Dr.)   19
Galileo   10, 11, 82, 194, 200,
                                           271, 293, 305
Gallaher, James   181v. 12
Galley, Edmund   70, 118
Gallo, Sam   196
Galway Election Petition   43
Gandhi, Mohandas Karamchand "Ma-
    hatma"   104, 214
Gardiner, William   180, 185, 273
Gardner, Alan Legge
    Henry Gardner v. Alan Gardner   172
Gardner, Obadiah (Sen.)   144
Gardner, William
    Union v. the States   268v. 4
Garmoyle: Viscount Garmoyle see
    Cairns, Arthur William (Vis-
    count Garmoyle)
Garnet, Harry   310v. 1
Garrison, William Lloyd   181v. 14
Gastle, Gordon   20
Gauba, K. L.   103
Gaudry, Nathalis   153, 309
Gaufridy, Louis   279
Gault, Gerald   306
Gautier, François   245
Gelfand, Michel   109
George V (King of Gt. Brit.)
    George V v. Mylius   295v. 6, 297
Gerard, John   310v. 1
Germain, George Sackville (1st Vis-
    count Sackville)   50
German Saboteurs see Dasch, George,
    et al.
German Submariners   304
Gerrald, Joseph   71v. 2
Ghose, Barinda Kumar, et al.   75, 262
Ghose, Tarit Kanti   262
Ghose, Tushar Kanti   262
Gibbons, Thomas
    Trumbull v. Gibbons   181v. 1
Gibbs, Edward Lester   178

Gideon, Clarence Earl   306
Giffard, Miles   101v. 1, 157
Gilbert, Pedro, et al   181v. 10
Gill, Charles   181v. 2
Gillars, Mildred   264
Gillespie, John Birks "Dizzy"
    Gillespie v. Nachbar   9
Gillette, Chester   178
Gilman, Ephraim   181v. 7
Gilman, Winthrop S. , et al.   181v. 5
Gilmour, Christina   240v. 2, 241, 249, 250,
                                         311

Gladstone, Henry & Viscount Gladstone
    Wright v. Gladstone   16, 75, 151, 152, 295v. 5
Glasgow Cotton Spinners   134
Godse, Nathuram V. , et al.   75, 169
Gontaut, Gabriel   18
Good, Sarah   182
Good, William   289
Goodere, Samuel (Capt.), et al.   51, 123, 280v. 2
Goodman, John   310v. 1
Goold, Vere & Marie   83
Gordon, Christian Frederich "Eric"
    Lady Gordon v. Christian Gordon   297
Gordon, George (Lord)   92v. 1
Gordon, Iain   101v. 1
Gordon, John William   101v. 2
Gordon, Lauden & Lockhart   34
Gordon-Cumming, Sir William
    Gordon-Cumming v. Wilson   45, 75, 129, 152, 260,
                                         295v. 4, 319

Gordon-Lennox, Ellen   29
Göring, Hermann   129
Göring, Hermann see also Nurem-
    burg Trials
Gorman, Edward   76
Gorman, William   89v. 1
Gorse Hall Murder see Howard,
    Cornelius
Goslett, Arthur Andrew   113, 184
Gottsdanker, Josephine
    Gottsdanker & Phipps v. Cutter
    Laboratories   9, 257
Goudie, et al.   297
Gould, Richard   183
Graham, Barbara   79
Graham, John Gilbert   251, 278

Grand, Digby   97v. 2
Gras, Jeanne Amenaide   153, 309
Grasty, Charles H., et al.   181v. 5
Graves, Thomas Thatcher (Dr.)   181v. 13, 223
Gray, Arthur   34
Gray, Henry Judd   83, 100v. 2, 178, 206,
                                             235, 258
Gray, Thomas & Hessie   298
Gray, William Thomas   113, 137, 173, 216
Great Plymouth Mail Robbery   12
Great Train Robbers see Biggs,
    Ronald Arthur, et al.
Great Warwickshire Scandal see Mor-
    daunt, Harriet Sarah (Lady)
Green, George   127
Green, Henry G.   181v. 17, 211
Green, Robert, et al.   36, 44v. 1, 280v. 3
Green, Shields   181v. 6
Green, Thomas (Capt.), et al.   247
Green Bicycle Mystery see Light,
    Ronald Vivian
Greenacre, James   33, 183
Greenberg, Samuel   222
Greenfield, Raymond & Frank   202
Greenwood, David   74, 147
Greenwood, Harold   88, 139, 157, 199, 285
Grenadier Guards   321
Grese, Irma   189, 227, 266v. 2
Grey, George, et al.   101v. 3
Grey, Ralph (3rd Lord Grey of
    Werke)   51
Grey Owl Estate Suit   168
Griffin, Thomas John   97v. 1
Griggs, Ronald   66
Groesbeek, Maria   28
Grondkowski, Marian   61
Gross, Louis   42
Grosvenor, Richard (1st Earl of
    Grosvenor)
  Grosvenor v. Cumberland   34, 317
Gruber, Jacob (Rev.)   181v. 1
Grubuxa, Mike   28
Grunzig, Otto   68
Grupen, Peter   117
Guardian Publications, Ltd.
  Agate v. Guardian Publications, Ltd.   15
Guay, Joseph Albert   217

Guerre, Martin see Du Tilh,
    Arnauld
Guiliano Gang Trial   252
Guinet, John Etienne   181v. 4, 302
Guiteau, Charles Julius   149, 165, 181v. 14
Gujarat Princes   103
Gully, James Manby (Dr.)   121, 180, 239, 241, 250
Gunn, Dennis   289
Gunpowder Plot see Fawkes, Guy,
    et al.
Gyani, Mushtaq Hussain   63

Haarmann, Fritz   86, 254
Hackleford Hospital (NYC), Dr.
    Michaels, et al.
  Wesley v. Hackleford Hospital,
    Dr. Michaels, et al.   175
Hackman, James (Rev.)   44v. 2, 51, 314
Hadfield, Albert   15
Hadfield, James   92v. 4, 163
Hadfield, John   40, 52, 93
Hadwen (Dr.)   221
Hafner, Bertha   126
Hagerman, Henry B.   181v. 14
Haggart, David   123, 247
Hahn, Andrée
  Hahn v. Duveen   3
Haigh, John George   4, 141, 173, 189, 207,
                                        226, 266v. 1, 294
Hakim Khan Murder   169
Hall, A. Oakley:
    1871 Trial   67
    1872 Trial   67
Hall, Carl Austin   251
Hall, Charlotte
  Rev. Hall v. Charlotte Hall &
    Richardson   172, 321
Hall, Eli H.   181v. 5
Hall, Frances Stevens   58, 149, 178, 208, 235,
                                        258
Hall, James William   66
Hall, Thomas   289
Hall, William   265
Hallinan, Terence
  Hallinan v. Brady, County of
    San Francisco & Gutierrez   269

Hamilton, Alexander (Gen.)
    Hamilton v. Frothingham   302
Hanion, John   181v. 3
Hanrahan, Edward V. & City of
    Chicago   269
Hanratty, James   6, 101v. 7
Hansen, Hans   181v. 14
Hapgood, Norman   295v. 4
Harchoux, Annette   18
Harding, Arthur (Dr.)
    Harper v. Harding & Kenyon   9
Hardy, Thomas   92v. 2
Hardy, William   265
Hare, William   8, 33, 37, 86, 123, 221,
                             239, 244, 296

Harley, Robert Paul, et al.   15
Harper, Harriet
    Harper v. Harding & Kenyon   9
Harries, Ronald   101v. 2, 157, 253
Harriman, Jane
    Harriman v. Dr. Deluca   175
Harris, Carlyle W.   120, 208, 215, 224, 272
Harris, Isaac _see_ Triangle Fire
    Case
Harris, Leopold Louis, et al.   111, 151, 307v. 1
Harris, Mary   165, 181v. 17
Harrisburg 7   10
Harrison, Henry   221
Hart, John   181v. 12
Hart, Nathan F.   223
Hartnett, Vincent
    Faulk v. Hartnett, Vincent &
        Aware, Inc.   212
Hartopp (Lady)
    Sir Charles Hartopp v. Lady Har-
        topp   297
Hartung, Mary   265
Hartzell, Oscar Merrill   295v. 3
Harvey   128
Harvey, Sarah   101v. 7
Harvey, Thomas
    Harvey v. Nariman   214
Hasson, Alan G. (Rev.)   21
Hastings, Warren   36, 148, 292
Haswell, Anthony   181v. 6, 302
Hatchard, John   284v. 1

Hatfield, John see Hadfield, John
Hatry, Clarence, et al.   74, 151
Hau, Karl   117
Hauer, John, et al.   62v. 2
Haugwitz-Reventlow (Count)
    Countess Haugwitz-Reventlow v.
        Count Haugwitz-Reventlow   15
Haupt, Hans Max, et al.   58
Hauptfleisch, Petrus Stephanus
        François   25, 29
Hauptmann, Richard Bruno   11, 57, 100v. 1, 148,
                                            161, 178, 233, 303
Havemeyer, William F.
    Kelly v. Havemeyer & Waterbury   67
Hawkins, Robert (Rev.)   51, 73
Hayes, Catherine, et al.   33
Haymarket Defendants:
    1886 Trial   98, 133, 208, 299
    1893 Trial   177
Hayward, George Frederick Walter   147
Haywood, William D.   57, 268v. 1
Hazeltine, Charles   181v. 11
Headfort (Marquis of Headfort)
    Massy v. Headfort   268v. 3-4
Heady, Bonnie Brown   251
Heaman, Peter   245
Hearn, Sarah Ann "Annie"   16, 88, 151, 253
Heath, Neville George Clevely   31, 61, 96, 140, 189,
                                            207, 226, 227, 288,
                                            294, 312

Hedges, Michael & John   92v. 4
Heirens, William   79, 231
Henderson, Jimmie   84
Henderson, Oran (Col.)   300
Hendrickson, John   35
Henfield, Gideon   181v. 4, 302
Henley, David (Col.)   62v. 2, 181v. 3
Henry, Toni Jo   231
Henry Frederick (Duke of Cumberland)
    Grosvenor v. Cumberland   34, 317
Hensey, Florence (Dr.)   52, 221
Henwood, Frank Harold   60
Hepper, William Sanchez de Pina   173
Herbert, Philip (5th Earl of Pem-
        broke)   44v. 1, 51, 73
Herbert Fuller (Ship) Mystery see
        Bram, Thomas Mead Chambers

Herold, David E.   181v. 8
Hersey, George C.   211
Hertzog, James Barry Munnik (Gen.)
    Fraser v. Hertzog   237
Hess
    Hess v. The Churchman   295v. 7
Hesse-Darmstadt Crown Jewels Theft
        see Durant, James W.
Hewet, John (Dr.)   310v. 1
Heys, Arthur   157
Heywood, Peter, et al.   50, 148
Hickman, William Edward   217
Hicks, Albert   181v. 14
Hicks, Lutien Roy   101v. 6
Hightower, William A.   155
Hilaire, Marcel   109
Hill, James   50
Hill, Sarah Althea   181v. 15
Hill, Anthony J. : Anthony Hill Will
        Contest   91
Hillary Hospital (NYC) & Dr. Wilson
    Borgmann v. Hillary Hospital &
        Dr. Wilson   175
Hinks, Reginald Ivor   158, 253, 307v. 2
Hirsche, Herman H. (Mrs.)   181v. 10
Hiss, Alger   56, 100v. 2, 176, 208,
                                                    257
Hoag, Thomas   181v. 4
Hoch, Johann   272
Hodges, John   181v. 10
Hodgson, James William   23
Hoffman, Harry L.   100v. 2, 120, 144, 222,
                                                    233
Hofrichter, Adolf (Lt.)   117
Holloway, John William   296
Holloway, Joseph   17
Holm, Eleanor
    Holm v. Rose   213
Holm, Johannes Gysbertus Faure
    Neethling v. Holm   237
Holman, Jacob   160
Holmes, Alexander William   181v. 1, 268v. 3
Holmes, Herman H.   153, 187, 295v. 8, 298,
                                                    313
Holyoake, George Jacob   59
Holzinger, John Conrad   95

Home, Daniel Douglas
   Lyon v. Home   295v. 4, 316
Hone, William   59
Honyman, Sir Richard Bemptde Johnson
   Elizabeth Honyman v. Richard
      Honyman   318
Hooper, Robert C.   181v. 3
Hopewell, John Henry   28
Hopkins, Raymond (Capt.)   300
Horne, John see Tooke, John Horne
Horne, William Andrew   273
Horsten, Akake, pseud.   227
Horton, Andrew, et al.   181v. 12
Houghton, Henry Frederick, et al.   101v. 7
House, LeRoy & Mrs. House   231
Houston, Margaret   289
How, David D.   181v. 6
Howard, Arthur, et al.   118
Howard, Bernard Edward
   Howard v. Bingham   92v. 4
Howard, Catherine (Queen of Henry
      VIII of England)   87, 284v. 1
Howard, Charles Francis (Earl of
      Wicklow)
   William Howard v. Charles Howard   172, 322
Howard, Cornelius   88, 185
Howard, Thomas (4th Duke of Norfolk)   310v. 1
Howard, William George
   William Howard v. Charles Howard   172, 322
Hubbard, Ruggles   181v. 14
Huberman, Gus   234
Huggins, John   284v. 2
Hughes, John W. (Dr.)   181v. 2
Hulme, Janet   101v. 2, 116, 254,
                 266v. 2, 294
Hulten, Karl Gustav   149, 312
Humbert, Frédéric & Thérèse   114, 148
Hume, Brian Donald:
   1950 Trial   301
   1959 Trial   101v. 6, 150
Hummel, Abe   195
Hunne, Richard   229
Hunt, Henry, et al.   48v. 2, 299
Hunt, Joseph   33, 123, 125, 135, 141,
                 148, 229, 296
Hunter, Benjamin F.   181v. 13

Hunter, Thomas   286v. 2
Huntington, Henry
   Huntington v. Lewis & Simmons   17
Hurd, Roosevelt Carlos (Sr.), et al.   301
Huss, John   293
Hutchinson, Anne   62v. 1, 208
Hutton, Barbara (Countess Haugwitz-
   Reventlow) see Haugwitz-
   Reventlow (Countess)
Hyams, Dallas Theodore & Harry
   Place   127, 298
Hyde, Bennett Clark (Dr.)   272

Icardi, Aldo (Lt.)   269
Iggulden, George William   216
Indian National Army Trial   104, 214, 262
Industrial Workers of the World
   (I. W. W.):
     1917 Trial   144
     1920 Trial   131
Ingersoll, Sarah   80
Insull, Samuel   56, 307v. 2
Iqbal, Mohammed   103, 106
Ireland's Eye Case see Kirwan, Wil-
   liam Burke
Irish Crown Jewels Theft   77
Irish Republican Army: I. R. A.
   Coventry Explosion see
   Barnes, Peter
Irwin, Robert   233
Israel, Harold   42, 177

"Jack Spot" Conspiracy see Comer,
   Jack, et al.
Jack the Painter see Hill, James
Jackson, Idonie Rubidge   22
Jackson, William (Rev.)   52
Jackson, William, et al.   280v. 4
Jacob, Audrey Campbell   166
Jacoby, Henry   148, 256
Jagado, Helène   309
James, Frank   181v. 11, 235
James, Robert S. see Lisenba,
   Major Raymond

Jayewardene, Lenduwa Lokuge	5v. 2
Jayne, Silas	13
Jefferds, Charles	72
Jeffries, Mary (Mrs.)	228
Jehovah's Witness Appeal	168
Jekhels, Kasper	81
Jelke, Mickey	150
Jennings, Emerson	130
Jennings, Herbert John	
Van Ryneveld v. Jennings	237
Jennison, Nathaniel	181v. 17
Jervis, Ernest Scot (Capt.)	320
Jesuit Trials	310v. 1
Jesus	82, 268v. 2
Joan of Arc	10, 11, 37, 82, 194, 200,
	293, 305
Jocelyn, Percy (Bp. of Clogher)	44v. 2
Jockey Club (Newmarket Heath)	
Chapman v. Jockey Club	128
Johnson, Alex	268v. 5
Johnson, Allen	165
Johnson, Andrew (Pres. of the U. S.)	10, 11, 82, 98, 133,
	268v. 3, 287
Johnson, Edward T. (Capt.)	268v. 8
Johnson, Frank (Maj.)	
Johnson v. Bulawayo Chronicle	237
Johnson, James A. see Fort Hood	
Three	
Johnson, John	181v. 2
Johnson, John A. "Dogskin"	80
Johnson, Mary (Mrs.)	70
Johnston, George (Maj.)	275
Jones, Albert	268v. 5
Jones, Arthur Albert	101v. 7
Jones, Bart Stephanus	81
Jones, Beverly W., et al.	181v. 3
Jones, Elizabeth Marina	61, 149, 312
Jones, Harold	54
Jones, Henry	97v. 2
Jones, Valentine	48v. 1
Jonesco, Barbu	
Jonesco v. Evening Standard	15
Joniaux (Mme.)	309
Jordan, Chester S.	196
Joyce, Angela	
Joyce v. Baring	15

Joyce, John   181v. 7
Joyce, Johnny   19
Joyce, William   87, 139, 260, 293,
                                           295v. 9
Judd, Samuel   181v. 3
Judd, Winnie Ruth   231, 234
Jumel: Eliza B. Jumel Will Case   68

Kadambur   4
Kakori Conspiracy   75, 262
Karanjia, R. K.   63
Kaur, Palvinder   169
Kaur, Rani Bhagwan   105
Kazi, I. K. (Dr.)   63
Kean, Edmund
    Cox v. Kean   228, 319
Kehoe, Patrick   220
Keith, Helen Watt   240v. 1, 249
Keith, William   240v. 1, 249
Keller, Edward   184
Kelley, John J. see Great Plymouth
    Mail Robbery
Kello, John (Rev.)   244, 249
Kelly, Edward   76
Kelly, John
    Kelly v. Havemeyer & Waterbury   67
Kelly, John R.   181v. 4
Kelly, Ned   11, 156
Kelly, Thomas (New Zealand Trial,
    1866)   289
Kelly, Thomas (Ireland Trial, 1936)   76
Kennedy, Kenneth   101v. 2
Kennedy, Roland Nicholas   97v. 1
Kennedy, Samuel J. (Dr.)   72, 215
Kennedy, William Henry   74, 138, 147, 148, 180,
                                           185, 199, 216, 312

Kennett, Ann   296
Kenniff, Pat & James   97v. 2
Kenniston, Laban & Levi   181v. 14
Kent, Constance   7, 8, 53, 123, 159, 224,
                                           238, 239, 241, 250,
                                           296, 309

Kent, Tyler   162
Kenyatta, Jomo   10, 11
Kenyon, Joseph P. (Dr.)
    Harper v. Harding & Kenyon   9

Keppel, Agustus (Adm.)   50
Kerr, James   245
Kerr, Thomas Andrew   22, 32
Kessler, Marshall (Dr.)
    Burke v. Kessler & Parkway
        General Hospital, Miami   236
Khan, Ameer   214
Khan, Hashmadad   214
Khan, Mohammad Nawaz   105
Khan, Said   103
Khan of Hoti Mardan   107
Kidd, Thomas I.   268v. 4
Kidd, William (Capt.)   36, 50, 129, 142, 148,
                                            208
Kihsori Case   106
Kinder, Helen Mary   7, 156
King, Robert (2nd Earl of Kingston)   51, 275
King, William Henry (Dr.)   298
Kingston: Duchess of Kingston see
        Pierrepoint, Elizabeth (Duchess
        of Kingston)
Kingston: 2nd Earl of Kingston see
        King, Robert (2nd Earl of King-
        ston)
Kinloch, Sir Archibald Gordon   319
Kinney, Hannah   181v. 17
Kirby, Richard (Capt.), et. al.   50
Kirkwood, James:
    Kirkwood v. Linlithgow Town
        Council   243, 246
    Rex v. Kirkwood   242, 246
Kirkwood, James Boyd   245
Kirwan, Bernard   77
Kirwan, William Burke   43, 179, 230, 238, 241,
                                            242, 250, 259
Kishori, Numtaz   103
Kitson, Linda
    Kitson v. Playfair   228
Kleinschrot, Conrad, et al.   95, 211
Knapp, John Frances & Joseph Jenkins   181v. 7, 211, 224,
                                            268v. 2
Knatchbull, John (Capt.)   314
Kneeland, Abner   181v. 13
Knights Templars   194
Knollys (Lt. Col.)
    Knollys v. Earldom of Banbury   92v. 4

Knorr, Frances   97v. 2
Knott, Hester Elizabeth   30
Knowles, Benjamin (Dr.)   282
Knowles, Gladys
    Knowles v. Duncan   316
Kocan, Peter   263
Konigsmark, Charles John (Count),
    et al.   34, 51, 65, 73, 180
Korematsu, Fred   306
Kotalawala, John   5v. 1
Kowalewski, Czeslaw   220
Kramer, Joseph   266v. 1
Krause, Frederick Edward Traugott
    (Dr.)   28, 297
Kretske, Norton I.   54
Kreuger, Alexander   195, 217
Krishna, Hare   262
Ku Klux Klan   181v. 9
Kuntze, Archie C. (Capt.)   84
Kylsant (Lord)   74, 128, 162

Labbé, Denise   109
Lady Chatterley's Lover (Novel)   101v. 7
Lafarge, Marie   309
Lafon, Thomas, Jr.   181v. 4
Lagu, Anant Chintaman (Dr.)   107
Laidlaw, William R.
    Laidlaw v. Sage   295v. 7
Laksmikantham Murder Case   4
Lamb, William (Viscount Melbourne)
    Norton v. Viscount Melbourne   295v. 10, 314
Lambert
    Lambert v. Levita   128
Lambert, John   92v. 2
Lambie, Helen (Witness)   193
Lamont, Corliss   176
Lamprecht, Gert du Plessis   32
Lamson, David   118, 179
Lamson, George Henry (Dr.)   49, 90, 123, 124, 140,
                                                  186, 210, 221, 255,
                                                  266v. 1, 296
Land League Conspiracy   43
Landon, William   181v. 7
Landru, Henri Désiré   2, 7, 37, 86, 148, 149,
                                                  161, 189, 195,
                                                  266v. 1, 294

Langley, John	181v. 7
Langton, Thomas	205
Langworthy, Edward	
Mildred Langworthy v. Edward	
Langworthy	319
Larocque, William J.	20
La Roncière, Emile de (Lt.)	154, 309
Larsen, John M.	144
Laski, Harold	
Laski v. Newark Advertiser	115, 128, 295v. 5
Latimer, Irving	122
Laubscher, Miemie	27
Laurie, John Watson	140, 239, 240v. 2, 241, 250
Lavictoire, Emmanuel	20
Lawes, Charles	
Belt v. Lawes	125, 314
Lawless, Valentine Browne (2nd Baron	
of Cloncurry)	
Baron Cloncurry v. Piers	172
Lawrence, Richard	181v. 3
Lawrence, Richard (Dr.)	
Mele v. Bright Star Hospital	
(NYC), Dr. Lawrence, et al.	175
Lawson, Leonard Keith	263
Laxmiprasannamamma, Yellamanchilli,	
et al.	63
Leany, Daniel	119
Lecca, Paul, et al.	252
Lecky, Dennis Edmond	61
LeDoux, Emma	155
Lee, Jean	116
Lee, John	53, 296
Lee, Maria	29
Lee, Thomas (Capt.)	280v. 3
Lefroy, Percy see Mapleton, Percy	
Lefroy	
Lehman, James H.	77
Lehman, Julius:	
1902 Trial	181v. 9
1903 Trial	181v. 9
Leisler, Jacob	62v. 1, 181v. 10
Lemmon, Jonathan	68
Le Neve, Ethel	292
Lennox, Mary (Lady)	
Lord Lennox v. Lady Lennox	172

Lenoir, Pierre   1
Leo Feist, Inc.
   Baron v. Leo Feist, Inc.   213
Leonard, Laurence, et al.   205
Leonski, Edward Joseph   166
Leopold, Nathan: Leopold & Loeb   57, 79, 100v. 2, 149,
                                              178, 195, 235, 294,
                                              303
Lesnier   118
Lespagne   118
Lester, Alfred   97v. 1
Lesurques, Joseph   65, 154
Levenson, Sarah Rachel   83, 246, 295v. 1, 314
Levita, Sir Cecil
   Lambert v. Levita   128
Levy, Howard Brett (Capt.)   84, 290, 304
Lewis & Simmons
   Huntington v. Lewis & Simmons   17
Ley, Thomas J.   66, 115, 139, 198, 256,
                                              312
Leyra, Camilo Weston   178
Liberace
   Liberace v. Daily Mirror
      Newspapers, Ltd.   152
Liebman, Hyman Balfour   24
Light, Ronald Vivian   111, 180, 187
Lilburne, John   78, 310v. 1
Lincoln, Ignatius Timothy Trebitsch   94
Lincoln Conspirators   299
Lincoln Conspirators see also Names
   of Individual Conspirators   299
Lineveldt, Gamat Salie   23, 28
Lingg, Louis, et al.   181v. 12
Linlithgow Town Council
   Kirkwood v. Linlithgow Town Council   243, 246
Linsell, Gordon Kenneth   38
Lisenba, Major Raymond   178, 217, 234
Lisle, Alice (Lady)   2, 44v. 1, 87, 125, 129,
                                              164, 280v. 1
Liverpool Licensing Committee
   Justices
   Liverpool Licensing Committee
      Justices v. Russell   297
Liverpool Bank Case see Goudie,
   et al.
Livingston, Jean (Lady Warriston)   249
Lockett, James, et al.   74

Loeb, Richard A. see Leopold,
    Nathan: Leopold & Loeb
London Times
    Parnell v. London Times   43, 260, 295v. 5
Long, James (Rev.)   214
Long, Kenneth R.   144, 308
Long Island Railroad
    Donelon v. Long Island Railroad   213
Longford (Lord)
    Purdon v. Lord Longford   43
Longworth, Theresa
    Longworth v. Yelverton   37, 43, 240v. 2, 247
Lonsdale, Gordon   101v. 7, 150
Loomis, Frank (Dr.)   122
Lord Haw-Haw see Joyce, William
Lotz, Nicholas Johannes   32
Loughans, Harold   61
Louis XVI (King of France)   11, 44v. 2
Lovat: Lord Lovat see Fraser,
    Simon (12th Baron Lovat)
Lowell, Jim   35
Lowenberg, Moses   68
Lowrie, John Watson   249
Luard, Charles Edward (Maj. Gen.)   282, 315
Lucas, Arthur   168
The Luddites   48v. 2
Lushington
    Tichborne v. Lushington   8, 94, 125, 129, 260,
                                            287, 295v. 3
Lusk, Grace   80, 181v. 14
Lyddane, Anne   165
Lydow, Patrick (Fusilier)   260
Lyles, Anjette   41
Lyman, Theodore   181v. 12
Lynch, Arthur Alfred   260
Lynch, Robert Bloss "Colonel"   127
Lyon, Fitzroy David (Lt.)
    Pickett v. Lyon   320
Lyon, Jane
    Lyon v. Home   295v. 4, 316
Lyon, Matthew   181v. 6, 302
Lyons, Lewis W.   283

Macdonald, Alexander Bain   240v. 1, 241, 249, 250
MacDonald, William   166, 263

Macdonell, Alastair Ronaldson (15th
      of Glengarry)   243
Macfarland, Daniel   35, 179
MacFarland, William Allison   272
Mackay, W. M.
   Mackay v. Philip   237
Mackcoull, James   240v. 2, 247
Mackenzie, Alexander Slidell (Capt.)   84, 181v. 1
Mackenzie, Compton   149
Mackie, Grace
   McMeckan v. Mackie   156
Mackinnon, Mary   243
Maclean, Ronald (Maj.)   31
Macleod, Gilbert   71v. 2
MacLeod, Hugh   240v. 1, 241, 247, 250
Macrae, Andrew George   78, 183
Macrae, Mary Jane
   Macrae v. Afro-American (News-
      paper) Co.   91
Madeley, Walter Bailey
   Farrar v. Madeley   237
Madras: Council of Madras   see
      Council of Madras
Magnuson, John   80
Mahesh   107
Mahon, Patrick Herbert   47, 113, 148, 173, 198,
                                              216, 232

Major, Ethel   146, 255
Makin (Mr. & Mrs.)   97v. 2
Malahide Mystery see   McCabe, Henry
Malcolm, Sarah   44v. 2
Malinowski, Henryk   61
Mallalien, Richard Louis   26, 30
Mallin, Theresa
   Robert Mallin v. Theresa Mallin   212
Malvy, Louis Jean   1
Manchester Martyrs see   Allen, Wil-
      liam Philip, et al.
Mancini, Tony   16, 112, 120, 151, 173,
                                              190, 253, 307v. 2

Mandrin, Louis   99
Manning, George F. & Maris   186, 296
Manson, Charles   161
Manster, Harry   196
Manuel, Peter Thomas Anthony   101v. 5, 174, 189
Mapleton, Percy Lefroy   184, 296

Mapp, Dollree
  Mapp v. Ohio Supreme Court   306
Mara, Tim
  Mara v. Tunney   295v. 7
March: Earl of March see Morti-
    mer, Roger (Earl of March)
Marchant, Charles   35
Margarot, Maurice   71v. 2
Mariam (Mother Superior)   252
Marie Antoinette (Queen of Louis XVI
    of France)   37, 44v. 2, 293
Mark & Phillis (Negro Slaves)   181v. 11
Mark Rothko Estate Suit   3
Markham, George (Rev.)
  Markham v. Fawcett   92v. 4
Marks, Conrad   181v. 11
Markus, Edward William   24, 25
Maroro   289
Marshall, William Martin   301
Martin, Halpe, et al.   5v. 2
Martin, Hymie   19
Martin, Susanna   182
Marvin, Charles Thomas   321
Marwood, Ronald Henry   101v. 6
Mary (Queen of Scots)   11, 36, 44v. 1, 129,
                                       148, 194, 287, 293,
                                       310v. 1
Marymount, Marcus (Sgt.)   101v. 6
Maskelyne, J. Nevil
  Colley v. Maskelyne   295v. 4
  Stollberg & Evans v. Maskelyne   295v. 4
Mason, Alexander Campbell   17, 312
Massy, Charles (Rev.)
  Massy v. Headfort   268v. 3-4
Mata Hari see Zelle, Margaretha
    Geertruida
Mathews, Arnold Monteath   103
Mathibe, Jacob   81
Matuska, Sylvester   117
Maubreuil: Marquis de Maubreuil   171
Maule, Thomas   62v. 1, 181v. 5
Mavrogordato, Theodore (Maj.)
  Berrange v. Mavrogordato   237
Maximilian (Emperor of Mexico)   293
Mayberry, David F.   181v. 2
Maybrick, Florence   37, 138, 148, 192, 203,

	204, 206, 254,
	266v. 2, 285, 309
Maylon, Arthur	15
Mazurkiewicz, Wladyslaw	150
Mazzerella, Vincenzo	126
McCabe, Henry	77
McCarthy, Joseph see Army- McCarthy Hearings	
McCarthy, Justin William	251
McClellan, Fred Athens	202
McConaghy, Robert	181v. 10
McDermott, Frederick Lincoln	66, 166
McDonald, John Edward	29
McElroy, James	181v. 12
McEvoy, Hugh, et al.	181v. 13
McGannon, William H. (Judge)	19
McGowan, Edward	181v. 15
McKeon, Matthew (Sgt.)	84
McLachlan, Jessie	145
McLeod, Alexander	181v. 7
McLoughlin, Jack	32, 81
McLucas, Lonnie	277
McManus, George C.	258
McMaster, F. W.	181v. 9
McMeckan, John	
McMeckan v. Mackie	156
McMillan, Margaret	108
McNaughton, Daniel	260
McPherson, Aimee Semple	292
M'Daniel, Stephen	280v. 4
M'Donald, John	245
M'Dougal, Helen	8, 239, 244
Mead, William	125
Meads, Albert West (Maj.)	103, 106
Meagher, Richard Denis, et al.	69
Medina, Ernest L. (Capt.)	13, 300
Meerut Conspiracy	75, 104, 262
Mège, Pierre	99
Meisner, David	20
Melbourne: Viscount Melbourne see Lamb, William (Viscount Melbourne)	
Mele	
Mele v. Bright Star Hospital (NYC), Dr. Lawrence, et al.	175
Melville: Lord Melville see Dundas, Henry (1st Viscount Melville)	

Melvin, James, et al.	181v. 13
Merrett, John Donald	47, 239, 244, 282, 311
Merrett, John Donald see also	
Chesny, Donald	
Merrifield, Louisa	101v. 1, 108, 146, 255
Merritt, Ann	49
Merryman, John	181v. 9
Messenger, Peter, et al.	310v. 2pt. 1
Messina, Alfredo	150
Meteor (Steamship)	209
Metro-Goldwyn-Mayer Pictures	
Youssoupoff v. MGM	128, 152, 162, 307v. 2
Metropolitan Vickers Co.	307v. 1
Meunier (Customhouse Officer)	18
Meyer, Claude Toto	28
Meyer, Henry C. (Dr.)	215
Meysenburg, Emil A.	181v. 9
Mezzara, Francis	
Palmer v. Mezzara	181v. 1
M'Guigan, John	248, 254
Miami Beach (City)	
Vega v. City of Miami Beach	236
Miami-Dade County	
Dillon v. Miami-Dade County	236
Miami-Dade County Jail	
Adams v. Miami-Dade County Jail	236
Robinson v. Miami-Dade County Jail	236
Miami-Dade County Sheriff	
Williams v. Miami-Dade County	
Sheriff	236
Miao, Chung Y.	120, 147
Michaels, Walter (Dr.)	
Wesley v. Hackleford Hospital	
(NYC), Dr. Michaels, et al.	175
Michel, Marie	309
Mignonette (Ship) see Dudley,	
Thomas (Capt.)	
Mikulicz, Joseph	277
Miles, Brynmor Eric (Capt.)	307v. 2
Miles, Donald Ernest see Oppen-	
heimer Jewels' Theft	
Millar, John S.	181v. 9
Miller, David John	14
Miller, Walter	183
Milligan, Lambdin P., et al.:	
1864 Trial	304
1866 Trial	268v. 3, 304

Mills, Herbert Leonard	253
Millsom, Albert	132, 180, 216
Millspaugh, Andrew Jackson	
Millspaugh v. Adams	68
Mindszenty, Joseph (Card.)	11, 305
Miranda, Ernesto	306
Missouri-Kansas-Texas Railroad Co.,	
et al.	
Edwards v. Missouri-Kansas-Texas	
Railroad Co., et al.	9
Mitchell, David Henry	14
Mitchell, John	181v. 11
Mitchell, John W.	181v. 9
Mitchell, Robert Hayes	181v. 9
Mitchell, Steve	85
Mitchell, William "Billy" (Gen.)	10, 84, 257, 304
M'Kean, James	243
M'Lachlan, Jessie	135, 185, 239, 244,
	266v. 2
M'Naughton, Daniel	163, 286v. 1
Mohun, Charles (Lord)	34, 36, 51, 129, 148,
	197, 292
Mohun, Hurree	105
Molineaux, Roland Burnham	149, 215, 224, 272
Monahan, Annie F.	272
Monkey Trial _see_ Scopes, John	
Thomas	
Monkhouse, Alan, et al.	307v. 1
Monmouth: Duke of Monmouth _see_	
Scott, James (Duke of Mon-	
mouth)	
Monrousseau, Louis	99
Monson, Alfred John:	
Monson v. Tussaud's	152
Rex v. Monson	239, 311, 315, 316
Montesi Scandal	292
Montgomery, James	42
Montgomery, John Burgh (Capt.)	314
Montgomery, Thomas Hartley	43, 319
Monvoisin, Maxime N.	
Favre v. Monvoisin	67, 268v. 5
Moodie, Duncan Donald	27
Mooney, Thomas J.	131, 176
Moore, Charles	183
Moore, John	181v. 13
Moore, Robert: 1799 Trial	302

Moore, Robert: 1953 Trial	220
Mora, Dennis see Fort Hood Three	
Mordaunt, Harriet Sarah (Lady)	
Sir Charles Mordaunt v. Lady Mordaunt	172, 295v. 9, 319
Mordecai, Noah M.	181v. 1
More, Sir Thomas (St.)	87, 284v. 1, 293, 305
Morey, William	157
Morgan, John Pierrepont	258
Morris, Elease	
Morris v. Saint Francis Hospital (Miami Beach)	236
Morris, John	181v. 2
Morris, William Charles	156
Morrison, Steinie	17, 94, 123, 132, 135, 138, 148, 187, 188, 191, 192, 195, 198, 203, 219, 282, 296
Morriss, Hayley	15
Mortimer, Roger (Earl of March)	87
Morton, Robert	28
Moscow Trials	82
Mossler, Candace "Candy"	85
Most, Johann	48v. 1
Motherwell, Larry Lord	165
Mount, Henry Clarke	156
Mount Rennie Case	69
Movie Times (Journal)	
Dass v. Movie Times	103, 106
Moxon, Edward	286v. 2
Mudd, Samuel A. (Dr.)	181v. 8
Muir, Thomas	71v. 1, 134, 245
Mukerian Dacoity	169
Mul Raj, Diwan	105
Mullane, William	
John Talbot v. Mary Talbot & Mullane	172
Muller, Franz	186, 296
Muller, Richard (Dr.)	150
Mullins, George see Mullins, James	
Mullins, James	53, 183
Munn, Daniel W.	268v. 6
Munnik, Jan Henry	
Botha v. Munnik	237
Munnik, Jan Willem Hendrik	24, 30
Murc, John (Lord of Auchindrayne), et al.	247

Murdaugh, John   160
Murray, James   54
Murray, William (Maj.)   121
Murtagh, Dennis & Derek   101v. 2
Muschet, Nicol   247
Musmanno (Justice)
    Musmanno v. Eldredge   91
My Lai Massacre see Calley, William
        L. (Lt.); Medina, Ernest L.
        (Capt.); Henderson, Oran (Col.)
Mylius, Edward Frederick
    King George V v. Mylius   295v. 9, 297

Nachbar, Joachim
    Gillespie v. Nachbar   9
Nair, Saukaran
    O'Dwyer v. Nair   103
Nairn, Katharine   123, 239, 240v. 1, 249,
                                             319
Nanavati (Com.)   105
Nariman, Khurshed
    Harvey v. Nariman   214
Nash, Patrick   205
National Textile Workers Union
        (Gastonia, N. C.)   131
Nawaz, Mohammed   4
Naylor, James   171, 197
Naylor, Rufe
    Naylor v. Central News Agency   237
Neagle, David   181v. 15, 287
Neebe, Oscar W., et al.   181v. 12
Neet, Joseph   181v. 14
Neethling, Johannes Henoch (Rev.)
    Neethling v. Holm   237
Nel, Dietrich Johannes Willem   31
Nelson, Earle   86
Nelson, John Henry   31
Neu, Kenneth   283
Neumann, Diedrich   35
New Hyde Park, N.Y., Board of Union
        Free School District see Board
        of Union Free School District,
        New Hyde Park, N.Y.
New York Negro Plot   62v. 1
Newark Advertiser
    Laski v. Newark Advertiser   128, 295v. 5

Newell, Susan   146
Newett, George
    Roosevelt v. Newett   295
Newington, Hannah   276
Newman, John Henry (Card.)   320
Newton, Huey P.   39
Ney, Michel (Marshal)   293
Nicholls, Albert Raymond Kenneth   31
Nichols, George Robert   97v. 1
Nicholson, William Lawrence Warren   28
Nicolaievna, Maria (Countess Tarnowska)   83
Nil Durpan Case see Long, James
        (Rev.)
Niles, George W.   68
Nodder, Frederick   141
Nolan, Charles   80
Norfolk: Duke of Norfolk see Howard,
        Thomas (4th Duke of Norfolk)
Norkott, Arthur, et al.   73
Norris (Justice)
    Bannerjee v. Norris   104, 262
North Berwick Witches Trial   247
Northampton Insurgents   302
Northrop (White Plains, N. Y. , Case)   68
Nortje, Jan Christian   25, 29
Norton, George Chapple
    Norton v. Melbourne   295v. 10, 314
Noxon, John F.   178
Nunn May, Alan   111
Nuremberg Trials see also Names
        of Individual Defendants
Nuremberg Trials   10, 11, 82, 98, 111, 151,
                                                200, 278, 301, 305

Oakland Seven Conspiracy   14
Oates, Titus   221
Obenchain, Madalynne   234
O'Brien, Jane   77
O'Brien, William Smith   286v. 1
O'Callahan, James F. (Sgt.)   84
O'Connell, Daniel, et al.   286v. 2
O'Dwyer, Sir Michael
    O'Dwyer v. Nair   103
Ogilvy, Katharine see Nairn, Katharine
Ogilvy, Patrick   249
O'Hare, Kate R.   181v. 13

Oka Indians' Trial   127
O'Kane, Timothy Joseph
    O'Kane v. Palmerston   318
O'Laughlin, Michael   181v. 8
O'Leary, Cornelius & Hannah   76
O'Loughlin, Pearl   60
Oliphant, James   243
Onufrejczyk, Michael   101v. 2
Oppenheimer, Julius Robert   82
Oppenheimer Jewels' Theft   28
Orpet, William   120, 272, 313
Orsini, Felice, et al.   159, 266v. 1
Orton, Arthur   8, 94, 209, 260, 287,
                                                295v. 3
Osborne, Florence Ethel   317
Osborne, John, et al.   298
O'Shea, David   76
O'Shea, Katherine
    William O'Shea v. Katherine O'Shea
        & Parnell   204
O'Shea, William   77
Osteopathic General Hospital (Miami)
    Boatman v. Osteopathic General
        Hospital (Miami)   236
Owen, Edgar   186
Oxford, Edward   33, 286v. 1
Ozolins, Vilis   101v. 5

Pace, Beatrice Annie   16, 151
Paine, Thomas   92v. 1
Paisley Witches Trial   247
Palmer, Aaron H.
    Palmer v. Mezzara   181v. 1
Palmer, George Charles Frederick   97v. 1
Palmer, Thomas Fyshe   71v. 1
Palmer, William (Dr.)   49, 53, 86, 90, 123, 136,
                                                148, 159, 210, 221,
                                                255, 266v. 1, 294,
                                                296
Palmerston, Henry John (P. M. of Gt.
        Brit.)
    O'Kane v. Palmerston   318
Panchenko (Dr.)   217
Pandes' Trial   4
Pandey, Benoyendra   4, 105, 262

Panther Torture Case see McLucas,
     Lonnie
Parke, Ernest
   Euston v. Parke   152
Parker, Frederick William   113, 173
Parker, Pauline   101v. 2, 116, 254,
                                        266v. 2, 294
Parker, Richard, et al.   38, 44v. 2, 50
Parkway General Hospital (Miami)
   Burke v. Marshall & Parkway
     General Hospital   236
Parnell, Charles Steward:
   O'Shea v. O'Shea & Parnell   204
   Parnell v. London Times   43, 260, 295v. 5
Parr, George, et al.   85
Parr, Laura   233
Parrott, George Charles   17
Parsons, Albert R., et al.   181v. 12
Parsons, William   51
Partapendra, Benoyendra   75
Patch, Richard   275
Patrick, Albert T.:
   1900 Trial   295v. 2
   1902 Trial   58, 215, 223, 295v. 2
Patterson
   Patterson v. De Volkstem (Journal) 237
Patterson, Gertrude Gibson   60
Patterson, Nan   178
Pattinson, Joseph Colin   27
Paul, Sir John Dean, et al.   317
Payne, Augustus   274
Payne, Lewis   181v. 8
Peace, Charles   37, 153, 187, 229, 259,
                                        296
Peacham, Edmund   310v. 1
Peake, Arthur Jefferson   15
Pearson, William Linsay see Oppen-
     heimer Jewels' Theft
Peasenhall Mystery see Gardiner,
     William
Peete, Louise   79, 234
Pegler, Westbrook
   Reynolds v. Pegler   213
Pelizzioni, Serafino   46, 70, 119, 179
Pell, Max   157
Peltier, Jean Gabriel   48v. 1, 65

Peltz, Greta	170
Peltzer, Leon	123
Pembroke: Earl of Pembroke see Herbert, Philip (5th Earl of Pembroke)	
Penge Mystery see Staunton, Louis & Patrick	
Penn, William:	
1670 Trial	65, 125, 229
1690 Trial	281
Penruddock, John (Col.)	284v. 1, 310v. 1
Pere, Hamiora	289
Perera, Singhone	5v. 1
Perfect, Henry	51
Perreau, Daniel & Robert	40, 93
Perrot, Sir John	310v. 1
Perry, Arthur	72, 157
Perry, James	92v. 2
Perry, John, et al.	52, 73, 280v. 3
Petiot, Marcel (Dr.)	167, 217, 252, 254, 266v. 1
Petri, Marie	217
Peytel, Sebastian	120
Peyton, Charles	126
Philip, John (Dr.)	
Mackay v. Philip	237
Philips, James	181v. 11
Phillips, Billy	13
Phillips, Clara	234
Phillips, John Stanley	15
Phillips, Lionel, et al.	81
Phillpot, Frank	289
Philp, Francis (Capt.)	
Wilberforce v. Philp	316
Pickett, Alfred John	
Pickett v. Lyon	320
Picton, Thomas (Gov. of Trinidad)	33, 48v. 1, 148, 284v. 2, 292
Pienovi, Lawrence	181v. 5
Pierrepoint, Elizabeth (Duchess of Kingston)	33, 37, 51, 65, 102, 129, 148, 180, 197
Piers, Sir John	
Lord Cloncurry v. Piers	172
Pigott, Richard (Witness)	191
Pike, Joseph	
Pike v. Beamish	45

Pimlico Mystery see Bartlett, Ade-
    laide
Pine, Edmond see Savage, Daniel
Pineau, Henry   259
Pinney, Charles (Mayor of Bristol)   286v. 2
Pivardière, Louis Charles de la   118, 279
Pizzino, Ted, et al.   122
Playfair, W. S. (Dr.)
    Kitson v. Playfair   228
Plunkett, William Conyngham
    Plunkett v. Cobbett   48v. 1, 92v. 4
Podmore, William Henry   187
Podola, Guenther Fritz Erwin   101v. 6, 163
Polliack, David   24
Pook, Edmund:
    Pook v. Crosland   292
    Rex v. Pook   185, 276, 292
Poole, Lyttleton S.   202
Poole, Peter   101v. 7
Pope, Ervin   118
Popish Plot   261, 310v. 2pt. 2
Porthole Case see Camb, James
Powell, Linda
    Powell v. Fagan   236
Powers, Caleb, et al.   58, 160
Powers, Gary   150
Pranzini, Karl   187
Praslin: Duke of Praslin see Theo-
    bald, Charles Laure Hugues
    (Duke of Praslin)
Pratt, Wilton (Dr.)   20
Prescott, Abraham   181v. 5
Prince, Richard Arthur   296
Prior, Tab, et al.   80
Pritchard, Edward William (Dr.)   8, 49, 90, 124, 139,
                                            145, 210, 239, 241,
                                            250, 255, 296
Probert, Albert   113, 173
Probst, Anton   268v. 4
Proctor, John   182
Profumo Affair see Ward, Steven
    (Dr.)
Provis, John
    Provis v. Smyth   230
Prynne, William   284v. 1
Pugh, Joseph, et al.   230

Puglise, James   126
Pulford, Joseph   181v. 5
Purdon, Wellington
    Purdon v. Longford   43
Purvis, Will   118

The Quakers   62v. 1
Queen, Peter   174
Quelch, John (Capt.), et al.   181v. 5
Quérangel Family   159
Quien, Gaston   1

Rachel (Mme.) see Leverson, Sarah
      Rachel
Radcliffe, William   80
Radich, Stephen   3
Radley, William see Oppenheimer
      Jewels' Theft
Radziwill, Katherine (Princess)   81
Rahim, Abdul   103, 106
Rahmani, Shamim   107
Raleigh, Sir Walter   44v. 1, 75, 87, 129, 171,
                              194, 280v. 1, 293,
                              310v. 1

Ramensky, Johnny   21
Ramsay, David   310v. 1
Rattenbury, Alma   7, 61, 140, 148, 193,
                              206, 266v. 1, 292,
                              312

Rattlesnake Murder see Lisenba,
      Major Raymond
Rauschmaier, George   95, 211
Ravaillac, Francis   44v. 1
Ravara, Joseph   302
Raven, Daniel   96
Rawlinson, William Jackson   22, 32
Ray, James Earl   85, 267, 303
Ray, Nirmal Kanta   262
Rayne, Richard   179
Read, James Canham   78, 184
Red Barn Murder see Corder, Wil-
      liam
Red Wing Carriers
    Burgel v. Red Wing Carriers   236

Redenbaugh, Joseph   227
The Regicides   171, 280v.1, 310v.2pt.1
Reichstag Fire Trial   82, 307v. 1
Reilly, James (D. A.), et al.   126
Renshaw, James (Lt.):
    1808 Trial   181v. 17
    1809 Trial   181v. 17
Revelstoke: Lord Revelstoke see
    Baring, Rupert (Lord Revel-
    stoke)
Reynolds, Charles B.   181v. 16
Reynolds, James (Dr.)   302
Reynolds, Quentin
    Reynolds v. Pegler   213
Rheeder, Margaret Elizabeth   27
Rhenston, Alan (Dr.)
    Alvaro v. Washington Hospital (NYC)
        & Dr. Rhenston   175
Rhode Island Judges
    Rhode Island General Assembly v.
        Judges of the Supreme Court 62v. 2, 181v. 4
Rice, John   93
Rice, William Marsh: The Wills of
    W. M. Rice   295v. 2
Richardson, Frank
    Hall v. Hall & Richardson   172, 321
Richardson, Grace   101v. 4
Richardson, John   229
Richeson, Clarence V. T.   272
Ricolo, Angela
    Ricolo v. Andrea Doria/Stockholm 9
Ridder, Victor F.
    Foerster v. Ridder   213
Ridge, Charles, et al. see Brighton
    Police Case
Riembauer, Francis Salis   95, 211
Rinaldi, Antonio   22, 32
Risk Allah, Habeeb:
    Rex v. Risk Allah   276
    Risk Allah v. Daily Telegraph   276
Robbins, Jonathan   181v. 7, 302
Robert   34, 279
Roberts, Frederick Thomas   61
Roberts, George   101v. 1
Roberts, Nathaniel W.   68
Roberts, Roland   27
Robertson, James Ronald   174

Robinson, Cecil John   41
Robinson, Henrietta   35, 181v. 11
Robinson, Herbert   17
Robinson, John   132, 148, 187, 232
Robinson, John & Sarah   181v. 4
Robinson, Sir Joseph Benjamin
    Robinson v. Cohen   237
Robinson, Michael
    Robinson v. Miami-Dade County Jail   236
Robinson, Richard P.   89v. 1, 181v. 12, 211
Robinson, W. A. (Rev.)   81
Robinson, William, et al.   181v. 1
Rodriguez, Roman   79
Rogers, LeRoy   202
Rogers, Silas   42
Roget, Isaac   181v. 11
Romney Picture Case see Huntington,
    Henry
Roosevelt, Theodore (Pres. of the U.
    S.):
    Barnes v. Roosevelt   295v. 7
    Roosevelt v. Newett   295v. 6
Roper-Curzon, Henry Francis (Lord
    Teynham)   317
Rose, Billy
    Holm v. Rose   213
Rosenberg, Julius & Ethel   10, 11, 55, 149, 176,
                                            227, 293, 303
Rosier, Prudent   68
Ross, Charles William   25, 26
Ross, Colin Campbell   116, 166
Rottman, Arthur   289
Roupell, William   229, 230
Rouse, Alfred Arthur   16, 47, 128, 135, 142,
                                            148, 151, 198, 219,
                                            232, 253, 266v. 1,
                                            312
Rowland, Walter Graham   118, 119, 218
Rowles, Snowy see Smith, John
    Thomas
Roy, Kumar Ramendra Narayan see
    Bhowal Sanyasi Case
Royal Mail Case see Kylsant (Lord)
Rubenstein, Pasach N.   268v. 4
Ruby, Jack   269
Ruest, Genereux   217

Rulloff, Edward H.   265
Rum & Coca-Cola (Song) see Leo
       Feist, Inc.
Rumbold, Freda   101v. 4
Rura, et al. see Mukerian Dacoity
Rush, Benjamin (Dr.)
     Rush v. Cobbett   181v. 6, 295v. 5, 302
Rush, James Blomfield   183
Ruskin, John
     Whistler v. Ruskin   3, 152, 295v. 5
Russ, Calvin   68
Russell, Earl (Lord)   197, 260
Russell, Sir Edward
     Liverpool Licensing Committee
       Justices v. Russell   297
Russell, George   157
Russell, Hannah   119
Russell, John: John Russell Will Case 268v. 7
Russell, Stephen   181v. 6
Russell, William (Lord)   44v. 1, 280v. 2
Ruth, Christian, et al.   181v. 11
Rutledge, Robert C. (Dr.)   231
Ruxton, Buck (Dr.)   16, 124, 138, 143, 148,
                                        151, 207, 210, 253,
                                        266v. 1, 312

Ryland, William Wynne   40, 93
Ryves, Lavinia Janetta Horton
     Ryves v. The Attorney General
       (Ryves claim as heir to Duke
       of Cumberland)   295v. 1

Saboteurs' Trial see Dasch, George,
       et al.
Sacco, Nicola: Sacco & Vanzetti   2, 10, 11, 57, 100v. 1,
                                        130, 148, 149, 176,
                                        177, 235, 271, 281,
                                        293, 303

Sackville, George (1st Viscount Sack-
       ville) see Germain, George
       Sackville (1st Viscount Sack-
       ville)
Sage, Russell
     Laidlaw v. Sage   295v. 7
Sah, Pyarelal   63
Saint Fergus Affair see Smith,
       William (Dr.)

Saint Francis Hospital (Miami Beach)
    Morris v. Saint Francis Hospital   236
Saint John, Frederick Berkely
    Saint John v. Fawkner   156
Salem Witchcraft Trials   10, 11, 62v. 1, 82, 235
Samas, David see Fort Hood Three
Samburu Trial   274
Sander, Hermann (Dr.)   251
Sandwene, Ntimane   24, 25, 28
Sandyford Mystery see M'Lachlan,
    Jessie
Sanford, John F.
    Scott v. Sanford   133, 181v. 13
San Francisco County
    Hallinan v. Brady, San Francisco
        County & Gutierrez   269
Sangret, August   312
Sapiro, Aaron
    Sapiro v. Ford   295v. 6
Sarret, Georges   307v. 1
The Satirist (Journal)
    Marquis of Blandford v. The Satirist   172
Sauer, Hans (Dr.)
    Sauer v. Standard and Transvaal
        Mining Chronicle   237
Saunders, John   245
Savage, Daniel   119
Savage, Richard   52
Savonarola   293
Scampton, Thomas   70
Scanlan, John   120
Scarpetta, Olga
    Scarpetta v. DeMartino   236
Schaeffer, George   181v. 11
Schaff, Philip   270
Schenck, John O. (Mrs.)   272
Schmidt, Abraham   95
Schönleben, Anna   95, 211
Schroeder, Irene   126
Schwab, Michael, et al.   181v. 12
Schwartz, Daniel, Sr. & Jr.   181v. 11
Schwartz, Harry   313
Schweitzer, William, et al.   122
Scopes, John Thomas   10, 11, 34, 82, 98, 130,
        144, 176, 271, 303

Scott, Dred:
    Scott v. Emerson   181v. 13

Scott v. Sanford	133, 181v. 13
Scott, James (Duke of Monmouth)	37
Scott, John, et al.	181v. 7
Scott, Leonard Ewing	41
Scottsboro Boys	10, 11, 131, 148, 176, 222, 233, 281, 306
Seale, Bobby G.	39, 290
Seaman, William	187
Sears, Roebuck & Co.	
Been v. Sears, Roebuck & Co.	236
Seddon, Frederick Henry	17, 37, 47, 74, 75, 90, 94, 132, 135, 148, 191, 232, 296, 297
Seeger, Donald	306
Selfridge, Thomas O.	181v. 2
Sellar, Patrick	134
Sellick, Diana	181v. 2
Seneviratne, Stephen	5v. 1
Servetus, Michael	194
Seth, Chandrakant	63
Seymour, Edward (Duke of Somerset)	310
Seymour, Harris, et al.	181v. 3
Seznec, Guillaume	120
Shahidganj Mosque, Lahore, India	104
Shankaracharya of Sharada Peeth	214
Shankaral, Lalo	63
Shanks, William F. G.	67
Sharon, William (Sen.)	
Sharon v. Hill	181v. 15
Sarah Sharon v. William Sharon	181v. 15
Shaw, Benjamin	181v. 14
Shaw, Clay	267
Shaw, William Bunting	
Williams v. Shaw	237
Shay, Mortimer	68
Shcharansky, Antoly	305
Sheares, Henry & John	89v. 1
Sheen, William	230
Shepherd, Clifford	42
Shepherd, William	54
Sheppard, John	33, 44v. 2, 229
Sheppard, Samuel (Dr.)	12, 170, 178, 251
Sheridan, Edward (Dr.)	221
Sherrick, John	127, 298
Sheward, William	183, 230, 276
Shiffert, Henry, et al.	181v. 11

Shipley, William Davis (Dean of St.
    Asaph)   92v. 1
Shirley, Laurence (4th Earl of Ferrers) 33, 44v. 2, 51, 89v. 1,
                                          102, 148, 180, 197,
                                          260, 278

Shirley, Washington Sewallis (9th Earl
    of Ferrers)
    Smith v. Earl of Ferrers   51, 242, 246, 319
Sickles, Daniel E.   34, 35, 181v. 12, 165,
                                          208, 268v. 7, 281

Sievier, Robert   128, 297
Simons, Leonard   181v. 8
Simons, Moses   181v. 1
Simpson, Ann K.   181v. 5, 268v. 6
Singh, Amrik, et al.   103, 106, 169
Singh, Bhagat, et al.   104, 262
Singh, Dharamvir   169
Singh, Gurbakhsh, et al.   169
Singh, Kartar, et al.   169
Singh, Maharaja Bhupendra 105
Singh, Raja Lal   214
Singh, Rana Birpal   103, 106
Singho, Baron   5v. 1
Sir Francis Drake Estate Swindle see
    Hartzell, Oscar Merrill
Sirhan, Sirhan Bishara   267, 303
Skinner, Hannah
    Allcard v. Skinner   315
Skirving, William   71v. 1
Slade, Henry (Dr.)   315
Slater, Oscar   42, 46, 83, 111, 119,
                                        123, 136, 143, 145,
                                        193, 239, 244, 266v.1

Sligo (Marquis of Sligo)   317
Slingsby, Sir Henry   310
Slovik, Eddie (Pvt.)   84, 304
Small, Frederick L.   217, 223
Smethurst, Thomas (Dr.)   49, 70, 119, 124, 142,
                                        210, 219, 221

Smiley, Frank H.   54
Smith, Alexander Howland 240v. 1, 247
Smith, Alfonso Francis Austin 282
Smith, Cameron, et al.   295v. 1
Smith, Charles   17
Smith, Christian   181v. 1
Smith, George Joseph   17, 47, 74, 86, 132, 135,

	137, 148, 203, 204, 232, 294, 312
Smith, Jim "Gipsy"	101v. 7
Smith, John Thomas (alias Rowles)	66
Smith, Joshua Hett	62v. 2, 181v. 6
Smith, Lawrence John	66, 115, 139, 198, 312
Smith, Madeleine	8, 37, 49, 123, 134, 136, 143, 145, 148, 180, 193, 224, 239, 254, 266v. 2, 278, 296, 309, 311
Smith, Martin Wessels	31
Smith, Mary Elder	240v. 2, 249
Smith, Mary Elizabeth Smith v. Earl of Ferrers	51, 242, 246, 319
Smith, Richard	181v. 5
Smith, William (Dr.)	230, 240v. 2, 244, 248, 249
Smyth, Sir John Provis v. Smyth	230
Snee, Helen	320
Snook, James Howard (Dr.)	231
Snyder, Robert M.	181v. 9
Snyder, Ruth	83, 100v. 2, 178, 206, 235, 258
Sobani, Begum Omar	107
Sobell, Morton	11
Socrates	10, 11, 34, 82, 148, 194, 200, 271, 293
Solomon, John, et al.	181v. 5
Somerset: Duke of Somerset see Seymour, Edward (Duke of Somerset)	
Somerset: Earl & Countess of Somerset see Carr, Robert (Earl of Somerset) & Frances (Countess of Somerset)	
Sörgel, John George	95
Soursas, Simone	109
Soutar, Charles	148, 240v. 2, 241, 249, 250
Southard, Elizabeth	181v. 2
Spangler, Edward	181v. 8
Spencer, Eliphalet M. S.	68
Spies, August, et al. see Haymarket Defendants (1886)	

Spock, Benjamin (Dr.) see Boston
      Five
Spooner, Alden   181v. 1
Spooner, Bathsheba, et al.   62v. 2, 181v. 2, 208
Sprague, Charles   181v. 4
Sprague, Preserved   181v. 14
Stafford, Edward (Duke of Buckingham)   310v. 1
Stahler, Henry, et al.   181v. 11
Standard and Transvaal MIning Chronicle
      Sauer v. Standard and Transvaal
            Mining Chronicle   237
Stanfield, Annie Amelia   148
Stanfield, Philip   51, 73, 240v. 1, 249
Stanfield Hall Murder see Rush,
      James Blomfield
Stanhope, Augustus (Lt.)   317
Stanley, Arthur Cromwell (Lt.)   25, 29
The Star (Newspaper)
      Chamberlain v. The Star   297
Starchfield, John   185
Staunton, Louis & Patrick   53, 83, 135, 191, 193,
                                           296
Stavisky Inquiry Commission   307v. 2
Stead, William Thomas   148, 295v. 9, 322
Stein, Harry   222
Steiner, Ludwig   95
Steinheil, Marguerite   117
Stengel, Otto, et al.   see German
      Submariners
Stent, Henry   52
Stephenson, David C.   56, 178
Stevens, Henry & William   149, 178, 208, 235, 258
Stewart, Alexander T.: The A. T.
      Stewart Will Case   295v. 2
Stewart, James   44v. 2, 135
Steyn, Hermanus, et al.   81
Stielow, Charles F.   42
Stirling: Earl of Stirling see Alex-
      ander, Alexander (claimed Earl
      of Stirling)
Stockdale, John   92v. 2
Stokes, Rose Pastor   181v. 13
Stollberg, Ernest
      Stollberg & Evans v. Maskelyne   295v. 4
Stone, William   92v. 3
Stoner, George Percy   7, 61, 140, 148, 193,
                                           206, 266v. 1, 292, 312

Stopes, Marie (Dr.)
   Stopes v. Sutherland   152
Story, John   268v. 5
Stourton, Charles (Lord)   51, 180, 229
Straffen, John Thomas   142, 163, 256
Strafford: Earl of Strafford   see
   Wentworth, Thomas (Earl of
   Strafford)
Strangeways, George (Maj.)   37
Stratton, Albert & Alfred   199
Stratton, George, et al.   see   Council
   of Madras
Streeter   54
Strumm, Franz Felix   185, 273
Strunk, Ira   268v. 5
Stuart, James   51, 286v. 1
Stuart, Mary see Mary (Queen of Scots)
Stuyvesant, John   181v. 7
Suffolk Witches Trial   280v. 1
Sugathadasa, Punchihewage   5v. 1
Sullivan, Joseph Thomas   289
Sumida Haruzo (Lt. Col.), et al.   278
Supple, Gerald Henry   156
Surratt, John H.   181v. 9
Surratt, Mary Eugenia   11, 55, 176, 177, 181v. 8,
                              235

Sutherland, Halliday Gibson (Dr.)
   Stopes v. Sutherland   152
Sutton, William Francis   251
Swanson, Maurice   21
Swart, Marthinus Erich Walter   31
Swartz, P. J. J.   81
Sweet, Ossian H. (Dr.)   98, 130
Sykes, Troisville   283
Symonds, Henry Delahy
   Troy v. Symonds   92v. 4

Talbot, Mary
   John Talbot v. Mary Talbot & Mullane   172
Talle, Tom   308
Tapner, Benjamin, et al.   33
Taracithio Gate wa Baragu   274
Taranath (Dr.)   4, 105, 262
Tarnowska: Countess Tarnowska see
   Nicolaievna, Maria (Countess
   Tarnowska)

Tawell, John   49
Tay Bridge Disaster Enquiry   134
Taylor, Louisa Jane   255, 273
Taylor, Percival Leonard   173, 216
Taylor, Peter Alfred
    Buchanan v. Taylor   316
Teapot Dome Cases   55, 149, 281
Tenants Harbor (Maine) Mystery   see
    Hart, Nathan F.
Terry, David S. (Judge):
    1856 Trial   181v. 15
    1888 Trial   181v. 15
Terry, Lionel   289
Terry, Sarah Althea   181v. 15
Terry, Victor John   101v. 7
Teynham: Lord Teynham   see   Roper-
    Curzon, Henry Francis (Lord
    Teynham)
Thacker, William J.   265
Thalreuter, James   95
Thanet: Earl of Thanet   see   Tufton,
    Sackville (9th Earl of Thanet)
Thaw, Harry   83, 100v. 1, 111, 268v.1,
                                                235
Thayer, Israel, Jr., & Isaac & Nelson   181v. 7
Theobald, Charles Laure Hughes (Duke
    of Praslin)   52, 89v. 1, 238, 279
Thistlewood, Arthur, et al.   see   Cato
    Street Conspiracy
Thomas, J. H.
    Thomas v. The Communist (News-
        paper)   17
Thomas, Vera   24
Thomas, Wilbert   64
Thompson, Edith Jessie   37, 47, 78, 83, 110, 113,
                                                119, 148, 149, 191,
                                                192, 207, 219, 232,
                                                278
Thompson, George   27
Thompson, John G.   268v. 2
Thompson, Louis   122
Thompson, Phil B., Sr., et al.   160
Thompson, Phil B., Jr.   160
Thompson, William   81
Thomson, Samuel   181v. 11
Thorne, Norman   47, 113, 148, 157, 162,
                                                173, 186, 191, 192,
                                                232

Thorne, Samuel John   289
Thornton, Abraham   44v. 2, 46, 65, 185, 211
Threadneedle Insurance Co.
    Empire Steamship Co. , Inc. v.
        Threadneedle Insurance Co.   15
Throckmorton, Sir Nicholas   87
Thurtell, John   8, 33, 44v. 2, 123, 125,
                                           135, 141, 148, 186,
                                           229, 296

Tichborne, Sir Roger
    Tichborne v. Lushington   8, 94, 125, 129, 260,
                                           287, 295v. 3

Tichborne, Sir Roger   see also   Orton,
        Arthur
Tijerina, Reies Lopez   257
Tilak, Bal Gangadhar   214
Tilton, Theodore
    Tilton v. Beecher   11, 268v. 1
Tirrell, Albert J.   196, 211
Titanic (Ship):
        Gt. Brit. Enquiry   297, 299
        U. S. Enquiry   299
Toal, Gerard   76
Toguri, Iva   264
Tokyo Rose   see   Toguri, Iva
Tolley, Cyril
    Tolley v. J. S. Fry & Sons, Ltd.   15
Tolputt, Gwendoline Mary   26, 30
Tone, Theobold Wolfe   284v. 1
Tonge, Thomas, et al.   310v. 2pt. 1
Tooke, John Horne:
        1777 Trial   284v. 1
        1794 Trial   92v. 3
Toomey, Alexander   245
Topi, Rutene   289
Toqué, et al.   1
Townley, George Victor   274, 314
Townsend, William   127, 298
Townshend, Frederick (Lord)   274
Toy, Crawford Howell   270
Tranby Croft Affair   see   Wilson,
        Arthur Stanley
Travers, Mary Josephine
    Travers v. Wilde   152, 191, 315, 322
Treffene, Phillip John   66
Tregoff, Carole   6, 170
Trenck, Frederick (Baron)   52

Triangle Fire Case	98, 208
Troiber, Michael	268v. 4
Troppmann, Jean Baptiste	86, 209
Trotsky, Leon	11
Troy, John Thomas	
Troy v. Symonds	92v. 4
Trucker, Robert, et al.	181v. 4
True, Ronald	113, 135, 137, 148, 256
Trumbell, John M.	
Trumbell v. Gibbons	181v. 1
Trunk Murders see Judd, Winnie	
Ruth; Mancini, Toni; Robinson,	
John	
Truscott, Steven	11
Tse-ne-gat	60
Tshozi, Skelemu	81
Tucker, Charles Louis	225
Tufton, Sackville (9th Earl of Thanet),	
et al.	92v. 3
Tuhiata	289
Tulley, Samuel	181v. 1
Tunney, Gene	
Mara v. Tunney	295v. 7
Turco, Arthur	277
Turner, Glenn Wesley	13
Turner, James (Col.), et al.	73, 280v. 1
Turpin, Richard	33, 44v. 2
Turpin, Ronald	168
Tussaud: Madame Tussaud & Sons	
Monson v. Tussaud's	152
Tweed, William M.	67
Twiss, Marie Pharialde Rosalind (Lady)	
Twiss v. Chaffers	316, 317
Twitchell, George S.	181v. 6
Twyn, John, et al.	44v. 1, 310v. 2pt. 1
Udderzook, William E.	224
Unger, August M. (Dr.)	54
United Airlines Co.	
DeVito v. United Airlines Co., &	
Douglas Aircraft Co.	9
U.S. Army: Army-McCarthy Hearings	
see Army-McCarthy Hearings	
U.S. Customs	
Brancusi v. U.S. Customs	3
Ury, John	181v. 1

Vacher, Joseph   167
Vacherot, Jeanne see Monrousseau,
   Louis
Vallandigham, Clement L.   181v. 1
Van Breda, Dirk Gysbert   81
Van Breda, Felix Leonard   31
Van Buren, Gordon   27
Vance, William   320
Vancrose, Fernand de   120
Vanderbilt, Gloria
   Vanderbilt v. Whitney   75, 307v. 2
Van der Merwe, Carel Aaron   81
Van der Merwe, Dina Dorothea   23
Vane, Sir Henry   310v. 2pt. 1
Van Meegeren, Henricus Antonius   3, 149
Van Niekerk, Andries Petrus   24, 25
Van Rensburg, Barend S.   29
Van Ryneveld, William Cornelius (Maj.)
   Van Ryneveld v. Jennings   237
Van Wyk, Stephanus Louis   24, 30, 118
Vanzetti, Bartolomeo see Sacco,
   Nicola: Sacco & Vanzetti
Vaquier, Jean Pierre   113, 128, 148, 216, 232
Vaux, Peter, et al.   154
Vega, Nobel
   Vega v. City of Miami Beach   236
Velaithan   5v. 1
Velonias, Stefanos   263
Verger, Jean-Louis   167
Vermaak, Herbert Vincent   30
Vermilya, Louise   272
Vestris (Ship) Investigation   295v. 6
Vidil, Alfred de (Baron)   318
Vigol, William   181v. 11
Villato, Francis   302
Vineyard, James R.   80
Vint, John, et al.   92v. 2
Vitalis, Marie   153
Vivian, John Cranch (Capt.)
   Vivian v. Lord Waterford   172
Voisin, Louis Marie Joseph   17, 94, 216, 232
Volunteers of America
   Better Business Bureau of Greater
      Philadelphia v. Volunteers of
      America   91
Von Arbin, Erik   195, 217

Von Gersdorf (Baron)
   Arnold the Miller v. Baron von
      Gersdorf   287
Von Ritter, Franz   181v. 13
Von Veltheim, Franz Ludwig   22, 81
Von Zell, Alfred Percival   22, 32

Wachs, George   95
Waddingham, Dorothea   146, 255
Waggoner, Charles Delos   235
Wagner, Louis   224
Wagner, John Adam   211
Wainewright, Thomas Griffiths   296
Wainwright, Henry & Thomas   53, 125, 135, 296
Waite, Arthur Warren (Dr.)   272
Waite, Raymond   220
Wakefield, Edward Gibbon, et al.   34, 286v. 2
Wakeman, Sir George (Dr.)   221
Walburger, Dotty   234
Waldo, Deloris   126
Walker, Jonathan   181v. 3
Walker, Thomas   92v. 2
Wall, Joseph (Gov. of Goree)   40, 48v. 1, 50, 148, 317,
                                  318
Wallace, Michael & Patrick   230
Wallace, William Herbert   7, 31, 70, 83, 88, 184,
                                 191, 192, 203, 204,
                                 206, 217, 254, 259,
                                 278
Walsh, Mike   68
Walters, Rowland, et al.   51
Wan, Ziang Sun   165, 202
Wanka, Alfred   27
Ward, Jane   127, 298
Ward, John   181v. 14
Ward, Matthews F.   160, 181v. 3
Ward, Steven (Dr.)   228
Ward, Thomas   181v. 4
Wardell, William Horsley   216
Waring, John U.   160
Warlick, Henry C. , et al.   181v. 9
Warner, Charles   248
Warriston: Lady Warriston see
      Livingston, Jean (Lady War-
      riston)

Warwick: Earl of Warwick and Holland
        see   Edward (Earl of Warwick
        and Holland)
Washington Hospital (NYC) & Dr. Rhen-
        ston
   Alvaro v. Washington Hospital &
        Dr. Rhenston   175
Waterbury, Nelson J.
   Kelly v. Havemeyer & Waterbury   67
Waterford (Lord)
   Vivian v. Lord Waterford   172
Watson, David F. (Maj.)   252
Watson, Ethan L.   67
Watson, James   48v. 2
Watson, John Selby (Rev.)   179, 317
Watson, Lindsay George (Lt. Col.)   252
Watt, Hugh   216
Watt, Newton   313
Watt, Robert (Capt.)   245
Weaver, James   173, 216
Webb, Madeline, et al.   231
Webster, John White   37, 123, 153, 178,
                                             181v. 4, 208, 211,
                                             224, 235

Webster, Kate   123, 187, 206, 266v. 2,
                                             296

Weeks, John   181v. 12
Weeks, Levi   181v. 1
Weems, William, et al.   181v. 10
Weerasamy   5v. 1
Weidmann, Eugen   158
Weir, Jean   240v. 1, 244, 249
Weir, Thomas (Maj.)   240v. 1, 244, 249
Wells, Warren   39
Wendel, John Gottlieb: The Wendel
        Claimants   295v. 2
Wentworth, Thomas (Earl of Straf-
        ford)   36, 44v. 1, 87, 148,
                                             268v. 7
Wentzel, George C.   42
Wesley, Albert
   Wesley v. Hackleford Hospital (NYC),
        Dr. Michaels et al.   175
West, Jerome   39, 64
West Port Murders see Burke, Wil-
        liam; Hare, William

Western Insurgents	181v. 11, 302
Westervelt, William H.	181v. 17
Weston, Henry	93
Weston, Richard	221
Westrich, Carl	22
Whakamau	289
Wharton, Elizabeth G.	165, 209
Wheaton, Eber	181v. 8
Wheeden, John	181v. 4
Wheeldon, Alice	36, 148
Wheeler, Mary Ann	80
Wheeler, Mary Eleanor (alias Mrs. Pearcy)	159
Wheeler, Mavis	101v. 2
Whelan, Patrick James	127, 211, 298
Whelpton, George	220
Whisky Insurgents see Western Insurgents	
Whistelo, Alexander	181v. 10
Whistler, James	
Whistler v. Ruskin	3, 152, 295v. 5
Whitesides, Thomas B.	181v. 9
Whiteway, Alfred Charles	101v. 1, 157, 288
Whitfield, John Leonard	19
Whitney, Gertrude	
Vanderbilt v. Whitney	75, 307v. 2
Whittaker, Johnson (West Point Cadet)	304
Wicklow: Earl of Wicklow see Howard, Charles Francis (Earl of Wicklow)	
Wielobycki, Dionysius (Dr.)	242
Wijeydasa Perera, Makawitage, et al.	5v. 2
Wilbar, William	
Wilbar v. Williams	181v. 7, 268v. 6
Wilberforce, Mabel	
Wilberforce v. Philp	316
Wild, Jonathan	33, 37, 44v. 2, 148, 229
Wilde, Jane F. (Lady)	
Travers v. Wilde	152, 191, 315, 322
Wilde, Mark	88
Wilde, Sir Oscar:	
Rex v. Wilde	10, 11, 129, 132, 293
Wilde v. Douglas	10, 11, 75, 129, 292, 295v. 5
Wilkes, John	148
Wilkins, Mary	
Blake v. Wilkins	43

Wilkins, Walter Keene (Dr.)   72
Wilkinson, Alec   220
Wilkinson, Benjamin R. (Dr.)   160
Wilkinson, Edward C. (Judge)   160, 181v. 1, 268v. 1-2
Wilks, Mark   295v. 10
Willgoss, Walter William   66
William Brown (Ship)   268v. 3, 287
Williams, B. W.
    Wilbar v. Williams   181v. 7, 268v. 6
Williams, Edward   116
Williams, Frederick Henry (Rev.)
    Williams v. Shaw   237
Williams, Isaac   181v. 12
Williams, John: 1911 Gt. Brit. Trial   128
Williams, John: 1921 U. S. Trial   281
Williams, John "Old Jack"   97v. 1
Williams, John Ambrose
    Williams v. Durham Clergy   286v. 2
Williams, Johnnie Lee
    Williams v. Miami-Dade County
        Sheriff   236
Williams, Thomas   273
Willner, Josephine   80
Wilson, Arthur Stanley, et al.
    Gordon-Cumming v. Wilson   45, 75, 129, 152, 260,
                                              295v. 4, 319
Wilson, Constance   230
Wilson, George (Dr.)
    Borgmann v. Hillary Hospital (NYC)
        & Dr. Wilson   175
Wilson, Howard, et al.   21
Wilson, James: 1867 New Zealand Trial   289
Wilson, James: 1917 Australia Trial   97v. 1
Wilson, Mary Elizabeth   101v. 5
Wilson, Sir Robert Thomas (Maj. Gen.)   50, 318
Winning Post (Newspaper)
    Wootton v. Winning Post   17
Winslow, Thomas   49
Winslow Boy see Archer-Shee,
        George
Winsor, Charlotte   179
Winston, Milton (Dr.)
    Enright v. Dr. Winston   175
Wirz, Henry (Capt.)   181v. 8
Wishart, George   34
Wittenburgh, Francis   181v. 1

The Wobblies see Industrial Workers
    of the World (IWW)
Wolcott, Harold   158
Wolkoff, Anna   162
Wolseley, Sir Charles, et al.   48v. 2
Wood, John   181v. 6
Wood, Robert   88, 110, 112, 132, 139,
                                          157, 180, 184, 190,
                                          191, 259
Woodfall, Henry Sampson   284v. 1
Woolahan, William   205
Wooldridge, Charles Thomas   296
Woolmington, Reginald   61
Wooton, Harry E.   181v. 17
Wootton, Richard
    Wootton v. Winning Post   17
Worrall, Robert   181v. 12, 302
Worrell, Edward D.   181v. 10
Wright, Peter (Capt.)
    Wright v. Lord Gladstone   16, 75, 151, 152, 295v. 5
Wright, Whittaker   94, 295v. 4, 297
Wynekoop, Alice (Dr.)   313

Yamashita, Tomoyuki (Gen.)   304
Yarham, Samuel   185, 230
Yates, Joseph Hollis, et al.   316
Yelverton, William Charles (Maj.)
    Longworth v. Yelverton   37, 43, 240v. 2, 247
York: Duke of York see Frederick
    Augustus (Duke of York)
Yorkshire Witch see Bateman, Mary
Young, Mary   33
Youssoupoff (Princess)
    Youssoupoff v. Metro-Goldwyn-
        Mayer Pictures   128, 152, 162, 307v. 2
Youtsey, Henry, et al.   160

Zafar, Bahadur Shah   214
Zelle, Margaretha Geertruida   293
Zenger, John Peter   10, 11, 62v. 1, 98, 177,
                                          181v. 16, 200, 208,
                                          229, 268v. 7
Zentner, George   268v. 4
Zola, Emile   114, 268v. 4
Zoldoske, Rose   80
Zwanziger, Anna see Schönleben, Anna

Subject List of Offenses and
Subjects of Trials*

Abduction
Abortion (Illegal Abortion)
Adultery
Adverse Possession
Affirmative Action
Arson
Assault
    See also   Indecent Assault
Assault with Intent to Kill   see
        Murder (Attempted Mur-
        der)

Bastardy
Bigamy
Blackmail   see   Extortion
Blasphemy
Body Snatching
Breach of Contract
Breach of Duty
Breach of Promise
Breach of Trust
Breach of Warranty
Bribery
Burglary

Challenge to a Duel
Child Custody
Communist Infiltration
    in Government
    see   Loyalty In-
    vestigations
Conspiracy
Contempt
Counterfeiting
Courts Martial
    See also   specific of-
        fenses, e. g. ,
        Treason; War
        Crimes
Criminal Libel
Cruelty
Cruelty to Animals

Debt Suits
Desertion   see   Military
        Desertion
Detention of Persons
Divorce
Draft Resistance
Due Process of Law

*For miscellaneous offenses, see end of Part III.

Duelling see Challenge to a
    Duel

Educational Equalization see
    Equal Educational Op-
    portunity
Embezzlement
Equal Educational Opportunity
Espionage
Eviction
Evolution in the Schools
Extortion

False Imprisonment
False Pretenses
Forgery
Fraud
Freedom of the Press

Habeas Corpus
Harboring
Heresy
Horse Stealing

Impeachment
Imposture
Indecent Assault
Inheritance and Succession
    See also Wills

Judicial Review
Jury Challenge
Jury Tampering

Kidnapping

Land Claims
Larceny
Libel and Slander

See also Criminal
    Libel; Seditious
    Libel
Liquor Offenses
Loyalty Investigations

Malpractice
Mandamus
Manslaughter
Matrimonial Suits
    See also Divorce;
    and specific
    charges, e. g. ,
    Adultery; Breach
    of Promise
Military Desertion
Military Draft Resistance
    see Draft Re-
    sistance
Murder
Murder (Attempted Mur-
    der)
Mutiny

Negligence
Neutrality (Breach of
    Neutrality)

Obscenity

Pandering
Perjury
Piracy
Plagiarism
Police Brutality
Pornography see Ob-
    scenity
Privateering (Illegal
    Privateering) see
    Neutrality (Breach
    of Neutrality)
Prohibition (Liquor Laws)

see   Liquor Offenses
Prohibition (Writ)
Prostitution

Rape
Religion in the Schools
Religious Liberty
Riot
Robbery

Sabotage
Search and Seizure
Sedition
Seditious Libel
Sexual Offenses
    See also Rape
Slander see Libel and Slander
Solicitation (of Chastity)

Spying see Espionage
Suffrage

Tariff Cases
Tax Evasion
Theft see Larceny
Torture
Treason

Unlawful Oath

War Crimes
Water Rights
Wills
Wire-Tapping
Witchcraft

Place of Trial and Defendant	Year of Trial	Source(s) Cited
ABDUCTION		
United States		
Seymour, Harris, et al.	1827	181v. 3
Westervelt, William H.	1875	181v. 17
ABORTION (ILLEGAL ABORTION)		
United Kingdom		
Collins, W. Maunsell (Dr.)	1898	221
ADULTERY		
Ireland		
Cloncurry: 2nd Baron of Cloncurry see Lawless, Valentine Browne (2nd Baron of Cloncurry)		
Headfort (Marquis of Headfort)		

ADULTERY (cont.)
    Massy v. Headfort   1804   268v. 3-4
    Lawless, Valentine Browne
    (2nd Baron of Cloncur-
    ry)
    Cloncurry v. Piers   c. 1800   172
    Massy, Charles (Rev.)
    Massy v. Headfort   1804   268v. 3-4
    Mullane, William
    John Talbot v. Mary
    Talbot & Mullane   1852   172
    O'Shea, Katherine
    William O'Shea v. Ka-
    therine O'Shea & Par-
    nell   1890   204
    Parnell, Charles Steward
    O'Shea v. O'Shea &
    Parnell   1890   204
    Piers, Sir John
    Cloncurry v. Piers   c. 1800   172
    Talbot, Mary
    John Talbot v. Mary
    Talbot & William Mul-
    lane   1852   172
  United Kingdom
    Bingham, Richard
    Howard v. Bingham   1794   92v. 4
    Bryce, Mabel
    Francis Bryce v. Mabel
    Bryce & Pape   1907   297
    Campbell, Colin (Lady)
    Lord Campbell v. Lady
    Campbell   1886   172, 319
    Caroline (Queen of George
    IV of Gt. Brit.)
    George IV v. Caroline   1820   48v. 2, 129, 197,
                                  292, 318
    Codrington, Helen Jane
    Henry Codrington v.
    Helen Codrington & An-
    derson   1864   318
    Cox, Robert Albion
    Cox v. Kean   1825   228, 319
    Crawford, Virginia Mary
    Donald Crawford v.
    Virginia Crawford &
    Charles Dilke   1886   172, 295v. 9, 314

Cumberland: Duke of
Cumberland see Henry
Frederick (Duke of
Cumberland)
Dilke, Sir Charles Went-
worth
Crawford v. Crawford
& Dilke   1886   172, 295v. 9, 314
Dunlo, Belle (Lady)
Viscount Dunlo v. Lady
Dunlo & Wertheimer   1890   320
Elgin, Thomas Bruce
(Earl of Elgin)
Elgin v. Ferguson   1806-08   172, 318
Ellenborough, Jane (Lady)
Lord Ellenborough v.
Lady Ellenborough   1830   318
Fawcett, John
Markham v. Fawcett   1802   92v. 4, 268v. 4
Ferguson, Robert
Elgin v. Ferguson   1806-08   172, 318
Gaiety Girl Divorce Case
see Bryce, Mabel
Grosvenor, Richard (1st
Earl of Grosvenor)
Grosvenor v. Cumber-
land   1770   34, 317
Hall, Charlotte
Rev. Hall v. Charlotte
Hall & Richardson   1873   172, 321
Henry Frederick (Duke of
Cumberland)
Grosvenor v. Cumber-
land   1770   34, 317
Howard, Bernard Edward
Howard v. Bingham   1794   92v. 4
Kean, Edmund
Cox v. Kean   1825   228, 319
Lamb, William (Viscount
Melbourne)
Norton v. Viscount
Melbourne   1836   295v. 10, 314
Markham, George (Rev.)
Markham v. Fawcett   1802   92v. 4
Melbourne: Viscount
Melbourne see Lamb,

ADULTERY (cont.)
    William (Viscount Mel-
      bourne)
    Norton, George Chapple

Norton v. Melbourne	1836	295v. 10, 314

    O'Kane, Timothy Joseph

O'Kane v. Palmerston	1864	318

    Palmerston, Henry John
      (P. M. of Gt. Brit.)

O'Kane v. Palmerston	1864	318

    Richardson, Frank
    Hall v. Hall & Richard-

son	1873	172, 321

    Vivian, John Cranch
      (Capt.)
    Vivian v. Lord Water-

ford	1869-70	172

    Waterford (Lord)
    Vivian v. Lord Water-

ford	1869-70	172

United States
    Adams, Seth

Millspaugh v. Adams	1865	68

    Beecher, Henry Ward
      (Rev.)

Tilton v. Beecher	1875	11, 268v. 1

    Brown, Orville H.

Brown v. Davidson	1860	68

    Dalton, Helen Maria
    Benjamin Dalton v.

Helen Dalton	1857	181v. 16, 268v. 5

    Davidson, Charles M.

Brown v. Davidson	1860	68, 268v. 7

    Favre, Theodore

Favre v. Monvoisin	1873	67, 268v. 5

    Forrest, Catherine
    Catherine Forrest v.

Edwin Forrest	1851-52	172

    Millspaugh, Andrew Jack-
      son

Millspaugh v. Adams	1865	68

    Monvoisin, Maxime N.

Favre v. Monvoisin	1873	67, 268v. 5

    Tilton, Theodore

Tilton v. Beecher	1874	11, 268v. 1

ADVERSE POSSESSION
  United States
    Streeter   1895-97   54

AFFIRMATIVE ACTION
  United States
    Bakke, Allan
      Regents of the Univer-
      sity of California v.
      Bakke   1974-78   306

ARSON
  Canada
    Oka Indians' Trial   1877-78   127
  France
    Duval, Clément   1888   18
    Vaux, Peter, et al.   1852   154
  United Kingdom
    Fergusson, Alan   1894   317
    Harris, Leopold Louis,
      et al.   1933   111, 151, 307v. 1
    Hill, James   1777   50
    Jack the Painter see
      Hill, James
    Scampton, Thomas   1875   70
  United States
    Ball, John   1817   181v. 7
    Clark, Stephen Merrill   1821   181v. 6
    Crockett, Simeon L.   1835   181v. 1
    Greenfield, Raymond &
      Frank   1924   202
    Larsen, John M.   1923   144
    Russell, Stephen   1835   181v. 6

ASSAULT
  Canada
    Disney, Daniel (Maj.)   1767   298
  France
    Doudet, Margarite Flore
      Célestine   1855   309
    Gaudry, Nathalis   1877   153, 309
    Gras, Jeanne Amenaide   1877   153, 309
    La Roncière, Emile de
      (Lt.)   1834   154, 309

ASSAULT (cont.)
    Ireland
        Delany, Thomas, et al.   1832   205
        Leonard, Laurence, et al.   1832   205
    United Kingdom
        Carrington (Lord)   1869   315
        De Vidil, Alfred (Baron)
            see   Vidil, Alfred de
            (Baron)
        Gray, Arthur   1721   34
        Kerr, James   1868   245
        Thanet: Earl of Thanet
            see   Tufton, Sackville
            (9th Earl of Thanet)
        Tufton, Sackville (9th Earl
            of Thanet), et al.   1799   92v. 3
        Vidil, Alfred de (Baron)   1861   318
        Watt, Robert (Capt.)   1868   245
    United States
        Ball, Lee   1925   202
        Corneilison, John J.   1884   160
        Crittenden, Thomas   1882   160
        Jennison, Nathaniel   1783   181v. 17
        McEvoy, Hugh, et al.   1824   181v. 13
        Moore, John   1824   181v. 13
        Morris, John   1816   181v. 2
        Pienovi, Lawrence   1818   181v. 5
        Poole, Lyttleton S.   1924   202
        Rogers, LeRoy   1925   202
        Simons, Moses   1818   181v. 1

BASTARDY
    United States
        Whistelo, Alexander   1808   181v. 10

BIGAMY
    United Kingdom
        Bristol: Countess of
            Bristol see   Pierre-
            point, Elizabeth (Duchess
            of Kingston)
        Feilding, Robert "Beau"   1706   51, 65, 280v. 3
        Kingston: Duchess of
            Kingston see   Pierre-

point, Elizabeth (Duchess
of Kingston)
Pierrepoint, Elizabeth
  (Duchess of Kingston)   1776   33, 37, 51, 65, 102,
                                         129, 148, 180,
                                         197

Russell, Earl (Lord)   1901   197, 260
United States
  Hoag, Thomas   1804   181v. 4

BLASPHEMY
  Palestine
    Jesus   29AD   82, 268v. 2
  United Kingdom
    Foote, George William,
      et al.   1882   59
    Holyoake, George Jacob   1842   59
    Hone, William   1817   59
    Moxon, Edward   1841   286v. 2
    Naylor, James   1656   171, 197
  United States
    Bell, Jared W.   1821   181v. 3
    Kneeland, Abner   1834   181v. 13
    Maule, Thomas   1696   62v. 1, 181v. 5
    Reynolds, Charles B.   1887   181v. 16

BODY SNATCHING
  United Kingdom
    Soutar, Charles   1882   148, 240v. 2, 241,
                                           249, 250

BREACH OF CONTRACT
  United Kingdom
    Allen
      Allen v. Flood   1895-97 297
    Empire Steamship Co.,
      Inc.
      Empire Steamship Co.,
      Inc. v. Threadneedle
      Insurance Co.   1925   15
    Ferrers: 9th Earl of
      Ferrers see Shirley,
      Washington Sewallis (9th
      Earl of Ferrers)

BREACH OF CONTRACT (cont.)
    Flood

Allen v. Flood	1895-97	297

    United Kingdom
      Langworthy, Edward
        Mildred Langworthy v.

Edward Langworthy	1883-87	319

      Maskelyne, J. Nevil
        Stollberg & Evans v.

Maskelyne	1898	295v. 4

      Shirley, Washington Se-
        wallis (9th Earl of
        Ferrers)

Smith v. Earl of Ferrers	1846	51, 242, 246, 319

      Smith, Mary Elizabeth

Smith v. Earl of Ferrers	1846	51, 242, 246, 319

      Stollberg, Ernest
        Stollberg & Evans v.

Maskelyne	1898	295v. 4

      Threadneedle Insurance Co.
        Empire Steamship Co.,
        Inc. v. Threadneedle

Insurance Co.	1925	15

    United States
      Mara, Tim

Mara v. Tunney	1930	295v. 7

      Tunney, Gene

Mara v. Tunney	1930	295v. 7

BREACH OF DUTY
    United Kingdom
      Pinney, Charles (Mayor

of Bristol)	1832	286v. 2

    United States

Bogart, Abraham	1856	181v. 5

      Hall, A. Oakey (Mayor of

N. Y.)	1872	67

BREACH OF PROMISE
    Ireland
      Blake (Lt.)

Blake v. Wilkins	1817	43

      Wilkins, Mary

Blake v. Wilkins	1817	43

United Kingdom
  Baring, Rupert (Lord
    Revelstoke)

Joyce v. Baring	1934	15

  Cairns, Arthur William
    (Viscount Garmoyle)

Finney v. Cairns	1884	314

  Duncan, Leslie Fraser

Knowles v. Duncan	1890	316

  Finney, Emily May

Finney v. Cairns	1884	314

  Fortescue (Miss) see
    Finney, Emily May
  Garmoyle: Viscount Gar-
    moyle see Cairns,
    Arthur William (Vis-
    count Garmoyle)
  Joyce, Angela

Joyce v. Baring	1934	15

  Knowles, Gladys

Knowles v. Duncan	1890	316

  Longworth, Theresa

Longworth v. Yelverton	1861-64	37, 43, 240v. 2, 247

  Revelstoke: Lord Revel-
    stoke see Baring,
    Rupert (Lord Revel-
    stoke)
  Yelverton, William Charles
    (Maj.)

Longworth v. Yelverton	1861-64	37, 43, 240v. 2, 247

BREACH OF TRUST
India

Sah, Pyarelal	1966	63

United Kingdom

Mackenzie, Compton	1932	149
Marvin, Charles Thomas	1878	321

BREACH OF WARRANTY
United Kingdom
  Huntington, Henry

Huntington v. Lewis & Simmons	1917	17

  Lewis & Simmons

BREACH OF WARRANTY (cont.)
    Huntington v. Lewis &
      Simmons   1917   17
    Romney Picture Case
      see Huntington, Henry

BRIBERY
    United Kingdom
      Bacon, Francis   1621   37
      Clarke, Mary Ann   1809   48v. 1
      Frederick Augustus (Duke
        of York)   1809   48v. 1
      York: Duke of York see
        Frederick Augustus
        (Duke of York)
    United States
      Butler, Edward   1902   181v. 9
      Darrow, Clarence   1912   268v. 8
      Gardner, Obadiah   1911   144
      Lehman, Julius   1903   181v. 9
      Meysenburg, Emil A.   1902   181v. 9
      Snyder, Robert M.   1902   181v. 9
      Worrall, Robert   1798   181v. 12, 302

BURGLARY
    Ireland
      Dowling, James   1832   205
      Woolahan, William   1832   205
    United Kingdom
      Sheppard, John   1724   33, 44v. 2, 229
      Turner, James (Col.)   1664   73, 280v. 1

CHALLENGE TO A DUEL
    United States
      Boott, William   1834   181v. 3
      Hooper, Robert C.   1834   181v. 3
      Renshaw, James (Lt.) 1809   181v. 17
      Wood, John   1818   181v. 6

CHILD CUSTODY
    United Kingdom
      Gordon, Christian Fred-
        erich "Eric"

Lady Gordon v. Christian Gordon	1903	297
United States		
Baby Lenore Case see		
DeMartino, Nick & Jean		
DeMartino, Nick & Jean		
Scarpetta v. DeMartino	1970	236
Scarpetta, Olga		
Scarpetta v. DeMartino	1970	236
Vanderbilt, Gloria		
Vanderbilt v. Whitney	1934	75, 307v. 2
Whitney, Gertrude		
Vanderbilt v. Whitney	1934	75, 307v. 2

CONSPIRACY

Australia		
Crick, William Patrick	1905	69
Meagher, Richard Denis, et al.	1895	69
Canada		
Banks, Harold Chamberlain	1964	168
Dorland, Albert	1930	20
The Doukhobors	1962	168
France		
Trenck, Frederick (Baron)	1794	52
Wilson, Sir Robert Thomas (Maj. Gen.)	1816	50, 318
India		
Ali, Maulana Mohammed & Maulana Shaukat	1921	214
Ghose, Barinda Kumar, et al.	1908-09	75, 262
Kakori Conspiracy	1926-27	75, 262
Meerut Conspiracy	1930	75, 104, 262
Shankaracharya of Sharada Peeth	1921	214
Ireland		
Forbes, James	1823	48v. 2
Land League Conspiracy	1881	43
O'Connell, Daniel, et al.	1843-44	286v. 2
Kenya		
Kenyatta, Jomo	1952	10, 11
South Africa		
Robinson, W. A. (Rev.)	1874	81

CONSPIRACY (cont.)
  United Kingdom
    Abrahams   1936   128
    Bowes, Andrew Robinson   1787   275
    Brighton Police Case   1958   101v. 5
    Bryan, Henry John, et al.   1951   253
    Canter, Ben, et al.   1955   101v. 3
    Cochrane, Thomas (Earl
      of Dundonald), et al.   1814   36, 48v. 2, 261,
                                     286v. 2
    Cochrane Johnstone, An-
      drew James   1814   275
    Comer, Jack, et al.   1955   101v. 3
    Grey, Ralph (3rd Lord
      Grey of Werke)   1682   51
    Harvey   1936   128
    Hedges, Michael & John   1803   92v. 4
    Hunt, Henry, et al.   1820   48v. 2, 299
    "Jack Spot" Conspiracy
      see Comer, Jack,
      et al.
    Krause, Frederick Ed-
      ward Traugott (Dr.)   1902   28, 297
    Miles, Brynmor Eric
      (Capt.)   1934   307v. 2
    Ridge, Charles, et al.
      see Brighton Police
      Case
    Snee, Helen   1876   320
    Vance, William   1876   320
    Walker, Thomas   1794   92v. 2
    Watt, Hugh   1905   216
    Wheeldon, Alice   1917   36, 148
  United States
    Abrams, Jacob, et al.   1918   268v. 6
    Amalgamated Woodworkers'
      International Union   1898   268v. 4
    Avery, Edward T.   1871   181v. 9
    Berrigan, Philip see
      Harrisburg 7
    Boston Five   1967   14
    Cain, Alfred E.   1970   39, 64
    Catonsville Nine   1968   14
    Chicago 7   1969-70   10, 303
    Childers, Sherod, et al.   1871   181v. 9
    Cochran, Tom   1973   13

De Leon, Ricardo	1970	39, 64
Eberle, Frederick	1816	181v. 12
Eyerman, Jacob	1799	181v. 11
Fall, Albert see Tea- pot Dome Cases		
Hanrahan, Edward V. & City of Chicago	1972	269
Harrisburg 7	1972	10
Jennings, Emerson	1935	130
Kidd, Thomas I.	1898	268v. 4
Ku Klux Organization	1871	181v. 9
Lincoln Conspirators	1865	299
See Also Names of Individual Conspirators		
McPherson, Aimee Semple	1926	292
Melvin, James, et al.	1810	181v. 13
Millar, John S.	1871	181v. 9
Milligan, Lambdin P.	1864	304
Mitchell, John W.	1871	181v. 9
Mitchell, Robert Hayes	1871	181v. 9
Munn, Daniel W.	1876	268v. 6
New York Negro Plot	1741	62v. 1
Oakland Seven Conspiracy	1969	14
Parsons, Albert R., et al.	1886	181v. 12
Payne, Lewis	1865	181v. 8
Roget, Isaac	1817	181v. 11
Ruth, Christian, et al.	1800	181v. 11
Schaeffer, George	1800	181v. 11
Schwartz, Daniel, Sr. & Jr.	1800	181v. 11
Shaw, Clay	1967	267
Shiffert, Henry, et al.	1800	181v. 11
Spock, Benjamin (Dr.) see Boston Five		
Stahler, Henry, et al.	1800	181v. 11
Surratt, Mary Eugenia	1865	11, 55, 176, 177, 181v. 8, 235
Teapot Dome Cases	1925-30	55, 149, 281
Thomas, Wilbert	1970	64
Troiber, Michael	1898	268v. 4
Warlick, Henry C., et al.	1872	181v. 9
West, Jerome	1970	39, 64
Whitesides, Thomas B.	1871	181v. 9
Zentner, George	1898	268v. 4

CONTEMPT
  India
     Gauba, K. L.   1942   103
     Ghose, Tarit Kanti   1935   262
     Ghose, Tushar Kanti   1935   262
  United Kingdom
     Daily Mirror Newspapers
        Ltd.   1949   115
  United States
     Debbs, Eugene Victor   1895   177, 295v. 7
     McMaster, F. W.   1872   181v. 9
     Radich, Stephen   1966   3
     Shanks, William F. G.   1873   67
     Terry, David S.   1888   181v. 15
     Terry, Sarah Althea   1888   181v. 15

COUNTERFEITING
  United States
     Gallaher, James   1820   181v. 12
     McElroy, James   1820   181v. 12

COURTS MARTIAL
  India
     Jervis, Ernest Scot
        (Capt.)   1866   320
     Meads, Albert West (Maj.)   1943-44   103, 106
  Jamaica
     Kirby, Richard (Capt.),
        et al.   1702   50
  Mexico
     Maximilian (Emperor of
        Mexico)   1815   293
  South Africa
     Carey, Jahleel Brendon
        (Capt.)   1879   315
  United Kingdom
     Byng, John (Adm.)   1757   50, 293
     Calder, Sir Robert (Vice-
        Adm.)   1805   50
     Germain, George Sack-
        ville (1st Viscount Sack-
        ville)   1760   50
     Grenadier Guards   1890   321
     Keppel, Agustus (Adm.)   1778   50

Lydon, Patrick (Fusilier) 1953 260
Sackville, George (1st Vis-
  count Sackville) see
  Germain, George Sack-
  ville (1st Viscount Sack-
  ville)
Stanhope, Augustus (Lt.) 1816 317
United States
  Adams, Paul (Sgt.) 1958 300
  Arnold, Benedict (Maj.
    Gen.) 1799 84, 181v. 6, 235
  Barron, James (Commo.) 1808 84
  Custer, George Arm-
    strong (Maj. Gen.) 1867 84
  Daley, Michael 1972 300
  Durant, James W. (Col.)
    & Kathleen B. 1946-47 252
  Fort Hood Three 1966 14
  Frémont, John Charles
    (Lt. Col.) 1847-48 299
  German Submariners 1944 304
  Henderson, Jimmie 1957 84
  Henley, David (Col.) 1778 62v. 2, 181v. 3
  Hesse-Darmstadt Crown
    Jewels Theft see
    Durant, James W.
  Hopkins, Raymond (Capt.) 1972 300
  Johnson, James A. see
    Fort Hood Three
  Kuntze, Archie C. (Capt.) 1966 84
  Levy, Howard Brett
    (Capt.) 1967 84, 290, 304
  Mackenzie, Alexander
    Slidell (Capt.) 1843 84, 181v. 1
  McKeon, Matthew (Sgt.) 1956 84
  Mitchell, William "Billy"
    (Gen.) 1925 10, 84, 257, 304
  Mora, Dennis see Fort
    Hood Three
  O'Callahan, James F.
    (Sgt.) 1956 84
  Renshaw, James (Lt.) 1808 181v. 17
  Samas, David see Fort
    Hood Three
  Slovik, Eddie (Pvt.) 1944 84, 304
  Watson, David F. (Maj.) c. 1950 252

COURTS MARTIAL (cont.)
    Whittaker, Johnson (West
       Point Cadet)   1880-82   304

CRIMINAL LIBEL
    France
       Zola, Emile   1898   114, 268v. 4
    India
       Long, James (Rev.)   1861   214
       Nil Durpan Case see
          Long, James (Rev.)
    South Africa
       Cartwright, Albert   1901   237
    United Kingdom
       Douglas, Alfred (Lord)   1923   152, 295v. 5
       Frankfort (Viscount)   1852   319
       Lambert, John   1793   92v. 2
       Perry, James   1793   92v. 2
       Vint, John, et al.   1799   92v. 2
    United States
       Bradstreet, Martha   1817   181v. 17
       Buckingham, Joseph T.   1824   181v. 14
       Garrison, William Lloyd   1830   181v. 14
       Grasty, Charles H., et al.   1893   181v. 5
       Hapgood, Norman   1906   295v. 4
       Lyman, Theodore   1828   181v. 12
       Simons, Leonard   1823   181v. 8
       Spooner, Alden   1818   181v. 1
       Walsh, Mike   1848   68
       Wheaton, Eber   1823   181v. 8

CRUELTY
    United Kingdom
       Sellar, Patrick   1816   134

CRUELTY TO ANIMALS
    United Kingdom
       Edalji, George   1903   42, 70, 118

DEBT SUITS
    United Kingdom
       Dennistoun, Ian (Lt. Col.)
          Dorothy Dennistoun v.
          Ian Dennistoun   1924   16

The Dustbin Case see
  Dennistoun, Ian (Lt.
  Col.)
Lyon, Fitzroy David (Lt.)
  Pickett v. Lyon   1890   320
Pickett, Alfred John
  Pickett v. Lyon   1890   320

DETENTION OF PERSONS
  United States
    Korematsu, Fred   1944   306

DIVORCE
  United Kingdom
    Catherine of Aragon
    (Queen of Henry VIII
    of England)
      Henry VIII v. Catherine 1529   10, 194
    Hartopp (Lady)
      Sir Charles Hartopp v.
      Lady Hartopp   1902   297
    Haugwttz-Reventlow (Count)
      Countess Haugwitz-
      Reventlow v. Count
      Haugwitz-Reventlow   1938   15
    Hutton, Barbara (Countess
      Haugwitz-Reventlow)
      see Haugwitz-Revent-
      low (Countess)
  United States
    Holm, Eleanor
      Holm v. Rose   1954   213
    Mallin, Theresa
      Robert Mallin v.
      Theresa Mallin   212
    Rose, Billy
      Holm v. Rose   1954   213
    Sharon, William (Sen.)
      Sarah Althea Sharon v.
      William Sharon   1884   181v. 15

DRAFT RESISTANCE
  United States
    Jones, Albert   1917   268v. 5

DRAFT RESISTANCE (cont.)
Miller, David John	1966	14
Mitchell, David Henry	1965	14
Seeger, Donald	1965	306
Story, John	1917	268v. 5

DUE PROCESS OF LAW
United States
Bell, James L.	1815	181v. 14
Escobedo, Danny	1960-64	306
Gideon, Clarence Earl	1962	306
Hubbard, Ruggles	1815	181v. 14
Miranda, Ernesto	1963?-66	306

EMBEZZLEMENT
India
Ahmed, Khwaja Nazir	1941	103

United Kingdom
Hasson, Alan G. (Rev.)	1971	21

United States
Caldwell, Oscar T.	1855	181v. 1
Childs, Nathaniel, Jr.	1849	181v. 2

EQUAL EDUCATIONAL OPPOR-
    TUNITY
United States
    Brown, Linda
Brown v. Board of Education, Topeka, Kansas	1954	306

ESPIONAGE
France
    Mata Hari <u>see</u> Zelle,
      Margaretha Geertruida
Zelle, Margaretha Geertruida	1917	293

India
Iqbal, Mohammed	1951	103, 106

Soviet Union
Powers, Gary	1960	150

United Kingdom
    Baillie-Stewart, Norman
(Lt.)	1933	307v. 1

Houghton, Henry Frederick,
   et al.   1961   101v. 7
   Kent, Tyler   1940   162
   Lonsdale, Gordon   1961   101v. 7, 150
   Marshall, William Martin   1952   301
   Wolkoff, Anna   1940   162
United States
   Abel, Rudolf Ivanovich   1957   150
   Beall, John Y.   1865   181v. 14
   Dasch, George, et al.   1942   149
   German Saboteurs see
      Dasch, George, et al.

EVICTION SUITS
   Ireland
      Galway Election Petition   1872   43

EVOLUTION IN THE SCHOOLS
   United States
      Monkey Trial see Scopes,
        John Thomas
      Scopes, John Thomas   1925   10, 11, 34, 82, 98,
                                    130, 144, 176,
                                    271, 303

EXTORTION
   United Kingdom
      Barnard, William   1758   51, 280v. 4
      Davies, Kathleen   1953   101v. 1
      Sievier, Robert   1928   128, 297
   United States
      Conforte, Joe   1949   42
      Cook, W. J.   1918   181v. 10
      Hirsche, Herman H.
        (Mrs.)   1918   181v. 10

FALSE IMPRISONMENT
   United Kingdom
      Kirkwood, James
        Kirkwood v. Linlithgow
        Town Council   1690   243, 246
      Linlithgow Town Council

FALSE IMPRISONMENT (cont.)
   Kirkwood v. Linlithgow
     Town Council   1690   243, 246
   United States
     Emerson, Irene
       Scott v. Emerson   1847-50   181v. 13
     Sanford, John F.
       Scott v. Sanford   1854   133, 181v. 13
     Scott, Dred
       Scott v. Emerson   1847-50   181v. 13
     Scott, Dred
       Scott v. Sanford   1854   133, 181v. 13

FALSE PRETENSES
   United Kingdom
     Charlesworth, Violet   1910   17
   United States
     Allen, Daniel K.   1818   181v. 12
     Dalton, James   1823   181v. 14
     Stuyvesant, John   1819   181v. 7

FORGERY
   France
     Harchoux, Annette   1887   18
   Germany
     Thalreuter, James   1826   95
   India
     Karanjia, R. K.   1952   63
   Netherlands
     Van Meegeren, Henricus
      Antonius   1947   3, 149
   United Kingdom
     Alexander, Alexander
      (claimed Earl of Stir-
      ling)   1839   286v. 1
     Ayliffe, John   1759   93
     Beswick, Frederick (Maj.)   1869   317
     Blackburn, Joseph   1815   93
     Cock, Henry   1802   93
     Dodd, William (Rev.)   1777   33, 36, 51, 65, 93,
                                     148, 314
     Fauntleroy, Henry   1824   40, 93
     Goudie, et al.   1902   297

Hadfield, John	1803	40, 52, 93
Hatfield, John see Hadfield, John		
Holloway, Joseph	1905	17
Liverpool Bank Case see Goudie, et al.		
Montgomery, John Burgh (Capt.)	1828	314
Perreau, Daniel & Robert	1776	40, 93
Pigott, Richard (Witness)	1889	191
Rice, John	1763	93
Robinson, Herbert	1905	17
Roupell, William	1862	229, 230
Ryland, William Wynne	1783	40, 93
Stirling: Earl of Stirling see Alexander, Alexander (claimed Earl of Stirling)		
Strumm, Franz Felix	1882	185, 273
Wainewright, Thomas Griffiths	1837	296
Weston, Henry	1796	93
Wielobycki, Dionysius (Dr.)	1857	242
United States		
Patrick, Albert T.	1900	295v. 2
Shepherd, Clifford	1935	42

FRAUD
France		
Humbert, Frédéric & Thérèse	1903	114, 148
India		
Mathews, Arnold Monteath	1937	103
Shankaral, Lalo	1950	63
New Zealand		
Howard, Arthur, et al.	1885	118
South Africa		
Radziwill, Katherine (Princess)	1902	81
United Kingdom		
Bailey, William (Rev.)	1843	317
Barber, William Henry	1844	8, 70
Beck, Adolf	1904	42, 46, 148, 154, 216, 219

FRAUD (cont.)

Bembridge, Charles	1783	92v. 2
Benson, Harry	1909	17, 199
Bond Street Mystery see		
Leverson, Sarah Rachel		
Booth, Handel	1915	128
Bottomley, Horatio	1922	17, 111, 132, 148,
		149, 295v. 3
Cameron, Cecil Aylmer		
& Ruby	1911	315, 317
Davison, Alexander	1808	48v. 1
Diamond Syndicate	1930	128
Easterby, George	1802	92v. 4
Francasal Case	1954	101v. 1
Hatry, Clarence, et al.	1930	74, 151
Home, Daniel Douglas		
Lyon v. Home	1868	295v. 4, 316
Jones, Valentine	1809	48v. 1
Kylsant (Lord)	1931	74, 128, 162
Leverson, Sarah Rachel	1868	83, 246, 295v. 1,
		314
Lyon, Jane		
Lyon v. Home	1868	295v. 4, 316
Paul, Sir John Dean, et		
al.	1855	317
Perfect, Henry	1804	51
Rachel (Mme.) see		
Leverson, Sarah Rachel		
Roper-Curzon, Henry		
Francis (Lord Teyn-		
ham)	1833	317
Royal Mail Case see		
Kylsant (Lord)		
Slade, Henry (Dr.)	c. 1876	315
Smith, Alexander Howland	1893	240v. 1, 247
Teynham: Lord Teynham		
see Roper-Curzon,		
Henry Francis (Lord		
Teynham)		
Wallace, Michael &		
Patrick	1841	230
Wright, Whittaker	1904	94, 295v. 4, 297
Yates, Joseph Hollis,		
et al.	1897	316
United States		
Bailey, Francis Lee	1973	13

Baker Estate Swindle see
  Smith, Cameron, et al. 1973   13
Brooks, Gertrude
  Brooks v. Conston   1945   91
Brown, Francis Wayland   1901   54
Clausen, William   1910   295v. 1
Conston, Harry
  Brooks v. Conston   1945   91
Fruehauf, Roy   c. 1954   212
Hartzell, Oscar Merrill   1933   295v. 3
Insull, Samuel   1934   56, 307v. 2
Niles, George W.   1850   68
Parr, George, et al.   1957   85
Roberts, Nathaniel W.   1850   68
Sir Francis Drake Estate
  Swindle see Hartzell,
  Oscar Merrill
Smiley, Frank H.   1901   54
Smith, Cameron, et al.   1936   295v. 1
Turner, Glenn Wesley   1973   13
Tweed, William M.   1873-75   67
Unger, August M. (Dr.)   1901   54
Waggoner, Charles Delos   1929   235

FREEDOM OF THE PRESS
  United Kingdom
    Carnan, Thomas   1779   92v. 1

HABEAS CORPUS
  India
    Khan, Ameer   1870   214
    Khan, Hashmadad   1870   214
    Singh, Rana Birpal   1943-44   103, 106
  United States
    Gault, Gerald   1964-67   306
    Lemmon, Jonathan   1852   68
    Merryman, John   1861   181v. 9
    Milligan, Lambdin P., et
      al.   1866   268v. 3, 304
    Thompson, John G.   1876   268v. 2
    Von Ritter, Franz   1816   181v. 13

HARBORING
  United Kingdom

HARBORING (cont.)
 Sligo (Marquis of Sligo)   1812   317

HERESY
 Czechoslovakia
  Huss, John   1441   293
 France
  Joan of Arc   1431   10, 11, 37, 82,
                                             194, 200, 293,
                                             305
  Knights Templars   1310   194
 Italy
  Bruno, Giordano   1592   194
  Galileo   1616-33   10, 11, 82, 194,
                                             200, 271, 293,
                                             305
  Savonarola   1498   293
 Switzerland
  Servetus, Michael   1553   194
 United Kingdom
  Hunne, Richard   1514   229
  Kirkwood, James   1695-97   242, 246
  Wishart, George   1545   34
 United States
  Bowne, Borden Parker   1904   270
  Briggs, Charles Augustus   1891-93   270
  Crapsey, Algernon Sidney   1906   270
  Quakers   1656-61   62v. 1
  Robinson, William, et al.   1659   181v. 1
  Schaff, Philip   1845   270
  Toy, Crawford Howell   1879   270

HORSE STEALING
 United Kingdom
  Turpin, Richard   1739   33, 44v. 2

IMPEACHMENT
 United Kingdom
  Dundas, Henry (1st Vis-
   count Melville)   1806   48v. 1
  Hastings, Warren   1788   36, 148, 292
  Melville: Lord Melville
   see Dundas, Henry (1st
   Viscount Melville)

United States
     Blount, William (Sen.)   1798-99   302
     Chase, Samuel (Judge)   1805   181v. 11
     Johnson, Andrew (Pres.
          of the U. S.)   1868   10, 11, 82, 98, 133,
                                                  268v. 3, 287

IMPOSTURE
     France
          Caille, Isaac de   see
               Mège, Pierre
          Collet, Anthelme   1820   99
          Dauphin Imposters   1799   99
          Du Tilh, Arnauld   1560   99, 279
          Guerre, Martin   see
               Du Tilh, Arnauld
          Mège, Pierre   1712   99
          Monrousseau, Louis   1659   99
          Vacherot, Jeanne   see
               Monrousseau, Louis

INDECENT ASSAULT
     United Kingdom
          Baker, Valentine (Col.)   1875   228, 317, 322
          Stead, William Thomas   1885   148, 295v. 9, 322

INHERITANCE AND SUCCESSION
     France
          De Champignelles, Rogres
               de Lusignan
               De Douhault v. De
                    Champignelles   1791   99
          De Douhault (Marchioness)
               De Douhault v. De
                    Champignelles   1791   99
     India
          Bhowal Sanyasi Case   1930-39   75, 262
          Roy, Kumar Ramendra
               Narayan   see   Bhowal
               Sanyasi Case
     Ireland
          Longford (Lord)
               Purdon v. Longford   1873-74   43
          Purdon, Wellington
               Purdon v. Longford   1873-74   43

INHERITANCE AND
SUCCESSION (cont.)
  United Kingdom
    Anglesea (Lord)
      Annesly v. Anglesea   1743   51, 129, 280v. 4,
                                                         287
    Annesly, James
      Annesly v. Lord Angle-
      sea   1743   51, 129, 280v. 4,
                                                         287
    Bainbrigge, Betty
      Thomas Parker Bain-
      brigge v. Betty Bain-
      brigge   1850   172, 230
    Banbury: Earldom of
      Banbury
      Knollys v. Earldom of
      Banbury   1813   92v. 4
    Berkeley, Frederick
      Augustus (5th Earl of
      Berkeley) (Berkeley
      Peerage Claim)   1799-   48v. 1
                                    1811
    Butler, Henry Edmund
      Pierce Butler v. Henry
      Butler   1854   172
    Day, Thomas
      John Day v. Thomas
      Day   1797   73
    Gardner, Alan Legge
      Henry Gardner v. Alan
      Gardner   c. 1823   172
    Howard, Charles Frances
      (Earl of Wicklow)
      William Howard v.
      Charles Howard   1869-70   172, 322
    Howard, William George
      William Howard v.
      Charles Howard   1869-70   172, 322
    Knollys (Lt. Col.)
      Knollys v. Earldom of
      Banbury   1813   92v. 4
    Lushington (Col.)
      Tichborne v. Lushington   1871-72   8, 94, 125, 129, 260,
                                                         287, 295v. 3
    Provis, John
      Provis v. Smyth   1853   230

Ryves, Lavinia Janetta
Horton
Ryves v. The Attorney
General   1866   295v. 1
Smyth, Sir John
Provis v. Smyth   1853   230
Tichborne, Roger
Tichborne v. Lushing-
ton   1871-72   8, 94, 125, 129,
                                                         260, 287, 295v.3

Wicklow: Earl of Wick-
low see Howard,
Charles Francis (Earl
of Wicklow)

JUDICIAL REVIEW
United States
Rhode Island Judges
Rhode Island General
Assembly v. Judges
of the Supreme Court   1786   62v. 2, 181v. 4

JURY CHALLENGE
United States
Gardner, William   1873   268v. 4

JURY TAMPERING
United States
Clough, Ebenezer   1833   181v. 3

KIDNAPPING
Canada
Meisner, David   1935   20
India
Gyani, Mushtaq Hussain   1950   63
Khan of Hoti Mardan   1912   107
United Kingdom
Anstruther, Sir Alexander 1720   243
Gordon, Lauden & Lock-
hart   1804   34
Wakefield, Edward Gib-
bon, et al.   1827   34, 286v. 2

KIDNAPPING (cont.)
   United States

Ancarola, Antonio	1879	181v. 3
Crowe, Pat	1905	295v. 8
Cudahy Case see Crowe, Pat		
Pulford, Joseph	1819	181v. 5
Robinson, John & Sarah	1837	181v. 4
Tijerina, Reies Lopez	1968	257
Wooton, Harry E.	1920	181v. 17

LAND CLAIMS
   India

Gujarat Princes	1953	103

   Southern Rhodesia

British South Africa Co.	1918	36

LARCENY
   Ireland

Irish Crown Jewels' Theft	1908	77

   South Africa
     Miles, Donald Ernest see
       Oppenheimer Jewels'
       Theft

Oppenheimer Jewels' Theft	1956	28

     Pearson, William Linsay
      see Oppenheimer
      Jewels' Theft
     Radley, William see
      Oppenheimer Jewels'
      Theft

   United Kingdom

Archer-Shee, George	1910	46, 111
Blood, Thomas (Col.)	1671	36, 148, 318
Fletcher, Susan	1881	320
Lockett, James, et al.	1913	74
Osborne, Florence Ethel	1891-92	317
Wild, Jonathan	1725	33, 37, 44v. 2, 148, 229

     Winslow Boy see Archer-
      Shee, George
   United States

Allison, Henry B., et al.	1851	181v. 4

Dayton, John	1817	181v. 2
French, Thaddeus P.	1827	181v. 2
Jones, Harold		54
Langley, John	1819	181v. 7
Philips, James	1819	181v. 11
Rosier, Prudent	1846	68
Weeks, John	1818	181v. 12

LIBEL AND SLANDER
Australia
Fawkner, John Pascoe

St. John v. Fawkner	1848	156

St. John, Frederick
Berkely

St. John v. Fawkner	1848	156

India
Banerjee, Surendranath

Banerjee v. Norris	1883	104, 262

Dass, Janki

Dass v. Movie Times	1949	103, 106

Harvey, Thomas

Harvey v. Nariman	1926	214

Movie Times (Journal)

Dass v. Movie Times	1951	103, 106

Nair, Saukaran

O'Dwyer v. Nair	1924	103

Nariman, Khurshed

Harvey v. Nariman	1926	214

Norris (Justice)

Banerjee v. Norris	1883	104, 262

O'Dwyer, Sir Michael

O'Dwyer v. Nair	1924	103

Ireland
Beamish, Richard Piggott

Pike v. Beamish	1894	45

Cork Card Case see
Beamish, Richard Pig-
gott

Pike, Joseph

Pike v. Beamish	1894	45

Travers, Mary Josephine

Travers v. Wilde	1864	152, 191, 315, 322

Wilde, Jane F. (Lady)

Travers v. Wilde	1864	152, 191, 315, 322

South Africa
Berrange, James Louis
Steyn

LIBEL AND SLANDER (cont.)

Berrange v. Mavrogor-
dato   1909   237
Botha, Louis (P. M. of
South Africa)
Botha v. Munnik   1915   237
Bulawayo Chronicle
Johnson v. Bulawayo
Chronicle   1905   237
Cagli, Augusto
Cagli v. Cape Mercury   1877   237
Cape Mercury (Newspaper)
Cagli v. Cape Mercury   1877   237
Central News Agency
Naylor v. Central News
Agency   1910   237
Cohen, Louis
Robinson v. Cohen   1911   237
DeVolkstem (Journal)
Patterson v. DeVolk-
stem   1917   237
Farrar, Sir George
Farrar v. Madeley   1913   237
Fichardt Ltd.
Fichardt Ltd. v. The
Friend   1915   237
Fraser, Colin
Fraser v. Hertzog   1911   237
The Friend (Newspaper)
Fichardt Ltd. v. The
Friend   1915   237
Hertzog, James Barry
Munnik (Gen.)
Fraser v. Hertzog   1911   237
Holm, Johannes Gysber-
tus Faure
Neethling v. Holm   1880   237
Jennings, Herbert John
Van Ryneveld v. Jen-
nings   1917   237
Johnson, Frank (Maj.)
Johnson v. Bulawayo
Chronicle   1905   237
Mackay, W. M.
Mackay v. Philip   1830   237
Madeley, Walter Bailey
Farrar v. Madeley   1913   237
Mavrogordato, Theodore (Maj.)

Berrange v. Mavrogor- dato	1909	237
Munnik, Jan Henry		
Botha v. Munnik	1915	237
Naylor, Rufe		
Naylor v. Central News Agency	1910	237
Neethling, Johannes Henoch (Rev.)		
Neethling v. Holm	1880	237
Patterson		
Patterson v. DeVolk- stem (Journal)	1917	237
Philip, John (Dr.)		
Mackay v. Philip	1830	237
Robinson, Sir Joseph Benjamin		
Robinson v. Cohen	1911	237
Sauer, Hans (Dr.)		
Sauer v. Standard and Transvaal Mining Chronicle	1887	237
Shaw, William Bunting		
Williams v. Shaw	1884	237
Standard and Transvaal Mining Chronicle		
Sauer v. Standard and Trans- vaal Mining Chronicle	1887	237
Van Ryneveld, William Cornelius (Maj.)		
Van Ryneveld v. Jen- nings	1917	237
Williams, Frederick Henry (Rev.)		
Williams v. Shaw	1884	237
United Kingdom		
Allen, Frances Caroline		
Allen v. Frayne	1915	162
Agate, James		
Agate v. Guardian Publi- cations Ltd.	1926	15
Austin, Charles		
Austin v. Disraeli	1838	65
Baccarat Scandal see Wilson, Arthur Stanley, et al.		

LIBEL AND SLANDER (cont.)
   Baillie, Thomas (Capt.)
     Board of Admiralty v.
     Baillie   1778   92v. 1
   Belt, Richard Claude
     Belt v. Lawes   1882   125, 314
   Blandford: Marquis of
     Blandford
     Marquis of Blandford v.
     The Satirist (Journal)   1838   172
   Board of Admiralty
     Board of Admiralty v.
     Baillie   1778   92v. 1
   Buchanan, Robert
     Buchanan v. Taylor   1876   316
   Cadbury, William
     Cadbury v. Evening
     Standard   1908   297
   Chaffers, Alexander
     Twiss v. Chaffers   1872   316, 317
   Chamberlain, Arthur
     Chamberlain v. The
     Star (Newspaper)   1901   297
   Chapman
     Chapman v. Jockey Club,
     Newmarket Heath   1936   128
   Chetwynd, Sir George
     Chetwynd v. Durham   1889   297, 319
   Cleveland Street Scandal
     see Parke, Ernest
   Cobbett, William
     Plunkett v. Cobbett   1804   48v. 1, 92v. 4
   Colborne, John (Capt.)
     Davis v. Colborne   1865   318
   Colley (Rev.)
     Colley v. Maskeleyne   1907   295v. 4
   Communist (Newspaper)
     Thomas v. Communist   1921   17
   Crosland, Newton
     Pook v. Crosland   1872   276
   Cumming, John
     De Ros v. Cumming   1837   45, 317
   Daily Mirror Newspapers
     Ltd.
     Liberace v. Daily Mirror
     Newspapers Ltd.   1959   152

Daily Telegraph
  Risk Allah v. Daily
    Telegraph   1868   276
Davis, Phineas
  Davis v. Colborne   1865   318
De Ros, Henry William
  (Lord)
  De Ros v. Cumming   1837   45, 317
Disraeli, Benjamin (P. M.
  of Gt. Brit.)
  Austin v. Disraeli   1838   65
Douglas, John Sholto
  (Marquess of Queens-
  berry)
  Wilde v. Douglas   1895   10, 11, 75, 129,
                                        292, 295v. 5
Durham (Lord)
  Chetwynd v. Durham   1889   297, 319
Durham Clergy
  Williams v. Durham
    Clergy   1822   286v. 2
Euston: Earl of Euston
  see Fitzroy, Henry
  (Earl of Euston)
Evening Standard (News-
  paper)
  Cadbury v. Evening
    Standard   1908   297
  Jonesco v. Evening
    Standard   1930   15
Fitzroy, Henry (Earl of
  Euston)
  Euston v. Parke   1890   152
Frayne
  Allen v. Frayne   1915   162
Fry, J. S. & Sons, Ltd.
  Tolley v. Fry & Sons,
    Ltd.   1928   15
George V (King of Gt.
  Brit.)
  George V v. Mylius   1911   295v. 6, 297
Gladstone, Henry & Vis-
  count Gladstone
  Wright v. Lord Gladstone 1927   16, 75, 151, 152,
                                        295v. 5
Gordon-Cumming, Sir
  William

LIBEL AND SLANDER (cont.)
    Gordon-Cumming v.

Wilson	1891	45, 75, 129, 152, 260, 295v. 4, 319
Guardian Publications Ltd.		
Agate v. Guardian Publications Ltd.	1962	15
Jockey Club (Newmarket Heath)		
Chapman v. Jockey Club	1936	128
Jonesco, Barbu		
Jonesco v. Evening Standard	1930	15
Kitson, Linda		
Kitson v. Playfair	1896	228
Lambert		
Lambert v. Levita	1936	128
Laski, Harold		
Laski v. Newark Advertiser	1946	115, 128, 295v. 5
Lawes, Charles		
Belt v. Lawes	1882	125, 314
Levita, Sir Cecil		
Lambert v. Levita	1936	128
Liberace		
Liberace v. Daily Mirror Newspapers Ltd.	1959	152
Liverpool Licensing Committee Justices		
Liverpool Licensing Committee Justices v. Russell	1905	297
London Times		
Parnell v. London Times	1888-90	43, 260, 295v. 5
Maskelyne, J. Nevil		
Colley v. Maskelyne	1907	295v. 4
Metro-Goldwyn-Mayer Pictures		
Youssoupoff v. MGM	1934	128, 152, 162, 307v. 2
Monson, Alfred John		
Monson v. Tussaud's	1895	152
Mylius, Edward Frederick		

King George V v. My-
    lius   1911   295v. 9, 297
Newark Advertiser
    Laski v. Newark Ad-
    vertiser   1946   128, 295v. 5
Newman, John Henry
    (Card.)
    The Queen v. Newman   1852   320
Parke, Ernest
    Euston v. Parke   1890   152
Parnell, Charles Steward
    Parnell v. London Times   1888-90   43, 260, 295v. 5
Philp, Francis (Capt.)
    Wilberforce v. Philp   1881   316
Playfair, W. S. (Dr.)
    Kitson v. Playfair   1896   228
Plunkett, William Conyng-
    ham
    Plunkett v. Cobbett   1804   48v. 1, 92v. 4
Pook, Edmund
    Pook v. Crosland   1872   292
Risk Allah, Habeeb
    Risk Allah v. Daily
    Telegraph   1868   276
Ruskin, John
    Whistler v. Ruskin   1878   3, 152, 295v. 5
Russell, Sir Edward
    Liverpool Licensing
    Committee Justices v.
    Russell   1905   297
The Satirist (Journal)
    Marquis of Blandford
    v. The Satirist   1838   172
The Star (Newspaper)
    Chamberlain v. The
    Star   1901   297
Stopes, Marie (Dr.)
    Stopes v. Sutherland   1923   152
Sutherland, Halliday Gib-
    son (Dr.)
    Stopes v. Sutherland   1923   152
Symonds, Henry Delahy
    Troy v. Symonds   1805   92v. 4
Taylor, Peter Alfred
    Buchanan v. Taylor   1876   316
Thomas, J. H.
    Thomas v. The Com-
    munist   1921   17

LIBEL AND SLANDER (cont.)
   Tolley, Cyril
      Tolley v. J. S. Fry &
        Sons, Ltd.   1928   15
   Tranby Croft Affair <u>see</u>
      Wilson, Arthur Stanley
   Troy, John Thomas
      Troy v. Symonds   1805   92v. 4
   Tussaud: Madame Tus-
      saud & Sons
      Monson v. Tussaud's   1895   152
   Twiss, Marie Pharialde
      Rosalind (Lady)
      Twiss v. Chaffers   1872   316, 317
   Whistler, James
      Whistler v. Ruskin   1878   3, 152, 295v. 5
   Wilberforce, Mabel
      Wilberforce v. Philp 1881   316
   Wilde, Sir Oscar
      Wilde v. Douglas   1895   10, 11, 75, 129,
                                     292, 295v. 5
   Williams, John Ambrose
      Williams v. Durham
      Clergy   1822   286v. 2
   Wilson, Arthur Stanley
      Gordon-Cumming v.
      Wilson   1891   45, 75, 129, 152,
                                     260, 295v. 4,
                                   319
   Winning Post (Newspaper)
      Wootton v. Winning Post 1913   17
   Wootton, Richard
      Wootton v. Winning Post 1913   17
   Wright, Peter (Capt.)
      Wright v. Lord Glad-
      stone   1927   16, 75, 151, 152,
                                   295v. 5
   Youssoupoff v. Metro-
      Goldwyn-Mayer   1934   128, 152, 162,
                                   307v. 2
  United States
    Afro-American (News-
      paper) Co.
      Macrea v. Afro-Ameri-
      can Co.   1958   91
    American Medical Associa-
      tion

Chattanooga Medicine
Co. v. American Medi-
cal Association   1916   295v. 4
Barnes, William, Jr.
Barnes v. Roosevelt   1914   295v. 7
Better Business Bureau
of Greater Philadelphia
Volunteers of America
v. Better Business
Bureau of Greater Phil-
adelphia   1937   91
Chattanooga Medicine Co.
Chattanooga Medicine
Co. v. American Medi-
cal Association   1916   295v. 4
Chicago Tribune
Ford v. Chicago Tribune   1919   295v. 6
The Churchman (Journal)
Hess v. The Churchman   1935   295v. 7
Cobbett, William
Rush v. Cobbett   1797   181v. 6, 295v. 5,
                                          302

Duveen, Sir Joseph
Hahn v. Duveen   1922   3
Faulk, John Henry
Faulk v. Aware, Inc.,
Hartnett & Johnson   1956   212
Foerster, Friedrich
Foerster v. Ridder   c. 1945   213
Ford, Henry
Ford v. Chicago Tribune   1919   295v. 6
Sapiro v. Ford   1925-27   295v. 6
Frothingham, David
Hamilton v. Frothing-
ham   1799   302
Gibbons, Thomas
Trumbull v. Gibbons   1818   181v. 1
Hahn, Andrée
Hahn v. Duveen   1922   3
Hamilton, Alexander (Gen.)
Hamilton v. Frothing-
ham   1799   302
Hartnett, Vincent
Faulk v. Aware, Inc.,
Hartnett & Johnson   1956   212
Havemeyer, William F.

LIBEL AND SLANDER (cont.)
    Kelly v. Havemeyer &
      Waterbury   1874   67
    Hess
      Hess v. The Churchman 1935   295v. 7
    Hill, Sarah Althea
      Sharon v. Hill   1883   181v. 15
    Kelly, John
      Kelly v. Havemeyer &
        Waterbury   1874   67
    Macrae, Mary Jane
      Macrae v. Afro-Ameri-
        can (Newspaper) Co. 1958   91
    Mezzara, Francis
      Palmer v. Mezzara   1817   181v. 1
    Newett, George
      Roosevelt v. Newett   1913   295
    Palmer, Aaron A.
      Palmer v. Mezzara   1817   181v. 1
    Pegler, Westbrook
      Reynolds v. Pegler   1955   213
    Reynolds, Quentin
      Reynolds v. Pegler   1955   213
    Ridder, Victor F.
      Foerster v. Ridder c. 1945   213
    Roosevelt, Theodore
      (Pres. of the U.S.)
      Barnes v. Roosevelt   1914   295v. 7
      Roosevelt v. Newett   1913   295v. 6
    Rush, Benjamin (Dr.)
      Rush v. Cobbett   1797   181v. 6, 295v. 5,
                                  302
    Sapiro, Aaron
      Sapiro v. Ford   1925-27 295v. 6
    Sharon, William (Sen.)
      Sharon v. Hill   1883   181v. 15
    Trumbell, John M.
      Trumbell v. Gibbons   1818   181v. 1
    Volunteers of America
      Better Business Bureau
      of Greater Philadelphia
      v. Volunteers of Ameri-
      ca   1937   91
    Waterbury, Nelson J.
      Kelly v. Havemeyer &
      Waterbury   1874   67

Wilbar, William
  Wilbar v. Williams   1845   181v. 7, 268v. 6
Williams, B. W.
  Wilbar v. Williams   1845   181v. 7, 268v. 6

LIQUOR OFFENSES
  United States
    Crary, George D.   1868   67
    Landon, William   1855   181v. 7
    Watson, Ethan L.   1868   67

LOYALTY INVESTIGATIONS
  United States
    Army-McCarthy Hearings   1954   177
    Fontana, John   1918   181v. 12
    Lamont, Corliss   1953   176
    McCarthy, Joseph see
      Army-McCarthy Hearings
    Oppenheimer, Julius Ro-
      bert   1954   82

MALPRACTICE
  United States
    Alvaro, George
      Alvaro v. Washington
      Hospital (NYC) & Dr.
      Rhenston   1965   175
    Boatman, Antoinette
      Boatman v. Osteopathic
      General Hospital, Miami   1974   236
    Borgmann, Margaret
      Borgmann v. Hillary
      Hospital (NYC) & Dr.
      Wilson   1958   175
    Bright Star Hospital (NYC),
      Dr. Lawrence, et al.
      Mele v. Bright Star
      Hospital, Dr. Lawrence,
      et al.   1964   175
    Burke, Jerry
      Burke v. Dr. Kessler
      & Parkway General
      Hospital, Miami   1973   236

MALPRACTICE (cont.)
  Carpenter (Dr.), et al.   1958 269
  Deluca, Walter (Dr.)
   Harriman v. Deluca 1962 175
  Enright, Larry
   Enright v. Winston 1961 175
  Fagan, Lewis (Dr.)
   Powell v. Fagan   1969 236
  Hackleford Hospital (NYC)
   Wesley v. Hackleford
   Hospital, Dr. Michaels,
   et al.   1960 175
  Harding, Arthur (Dr.)
   Harper v. Harding &
   Kenyon   1956 9
  Harper, Harriet
   Harper v. Harding &
   Kenyon   1956 9
  Harriman, Jane
   Harriman v. Dr. Deluca 1962 175
  Hillary Hospital (NYC)
   Borgmann v. Hillary
   Hospital & Dr. Wilson 1958 175
  Kenyon, Joseph P. (Dr.)
   Harper v. Harding &
   Kenyon   1956 9
  Kessler, Marshall (Dr.)
   Burke v. Kessler &
   Parkway General Hospi-
   tal, Miami   1973 236
  Lawrence, Richard (Dr.)
   Mele v. Bright Star
   Hospital (NYC), Dr.
   Lawrence, et al.   1964 175
  Mele
   Mele v. Bright Star
   Hospital (NYC), Dr.
   Lawrence, et al.   1964 175
  Michaels, Walter (Dr.)
   Wesley v. Hackleford
   Hospital (NYC), Dr.
   Michaels, et al.   1960 175
  Morris, Elease
   Morris v. St. Francis
   Hospital (Miami Beach) 1974 236
  Osteopathic General Hos-
   pital (Miami)

Boatman v. Osteopathic General Hospital	1974	236
Parkway General Hospital (Miami)		
Burke v. Marshall & Parkway General Hospital	1973	236
Powell, Linda		
Powell v. Fagan	1969	236
Rhenston, Alan (Dr.)		
Alvaro v. Washington Hospital (NYC) & Dr. Rhenston	1965	175
St. Francis Hospital (Miami Beach)		
Morris v. St. Francis Hospital	1974	236
Washington Hospital (NYC) & Dr. Rhenston		
Alvaro v. Washington Hospital & Dr. Rhenston	1965	175
Wesley, Albert		
Wesley v. Hackleford Hospital (NYC), Dr. Michaels, et al.	1960	175
Wilson, George (Dr.)		
Borgmann v. Hillary Hospital (NYC) & Dr. Wilson	1958	175
Winston, Milton (Dr.)		
Enright v. Dr. Winston	1961	175

MANDAMUS
United States
Eldredge, Laurence H.		
Musmanno v. Eldredge	1954	91
Musmanno (Justice)		
Musmanno v. Eldredge	1954	91

MANSLAUGHTER
India
Kazi, I. K. (Dr.)	1961	63
United Kingdom		
De Clifford (Lord	1935	295v. 8

MANSLAUGHTER (cont.)
    Ford, Arthur Kendrich   1954   255
    Hadwen (Dr.)   1924   221
    United States
        Arbuckle, Roscoe "Fatty"   1922   231, 268v. 8
        Blanck, Max see Tri-
          angle Fire Case
        Burke, Francis   1832   181v. 4
        Coburn, Edward O.   1856   181v. 16
        Dalton, Benjamin F.   1856   181v. 16
        Darnes, William P.   1840   181v. 16
        Harris, Isaac see Tri-
          angle Fire Case
        Holmes, Alexander William 1842   181v. 1, 268v. 3
        Triangle Fire Case   1912   98, 208

MATRIMONIAL SUITS
    United Kingdom
        Euston: Countess of
          Euston see Fitzroy,
          Kate Walsh (Countess
          of Euston)
        Fitzroy, Kate Walsh
          (Countess of Euston)
          Earl of Euston v. Count-
          ess of Euston   1884   172, 314
        Great Warwickshire Scan-
          dal see Mordaunt,
          Harriet Sarah (Lady)
        Honyman, Sir Richard
          Bemptde Johnson
          Elizabeth Honyman v.
          Richard Honyman   1825-31 318
        Lennox, Mary (Lady)
          Lord Lennox v. Lady
          Lennox   1831   172
        Mordaunt, Harriet Sarah
          (Lady)
          Sir Charles Mordaunt v.
          Lady Mordaunt   1869-70 172, 295v. 9, 319
    United States
        Browning, Edward W.
          Frances "Peaches"
          Browning v. Edward
          Browning   1927   258

MILITARY DESERTION
  United States
    Slovik, Eddie (Pvt.)   1944   84, 304

MURDER
  Algeria

Charles, Henri	1888	259
Doineau, Auguste (Capt.)	1857	274

  Australia

Abbott, William Henry	1951	166
Agostini, Antonio	1944	66
Bailey, Raymond John	1958	66, 166
Bertrand, Henry Louis	1865	7, 97v. 1, 156
Bradley, Stephen Leslie	1960	166
Brown, John Whelan	1959	66
Butler, Frank	1897	97v. 2
Coulter, William	1926	66
Craig, Eric Roland	1933	116
Deeming, Frederick Bailey	1892	27, 28, 86, 97v. 2, 184
Franz, Frank	1916	97v. 1
Grand, Digby	1903	97v. 2
Griffin, Thomas John	1867	97v. 1
Griggs, Ronald	1928	66
Hall, James William	1952	66
Jacob, Audrey Campbell	1925	166
Jones, Henry	1903	97v. 2
Kelly, Ned	1880	11, 156
Kennedy, Roland Nicholas	1916	97v. 1
Kenniff, Pat & James	1902	97v. 2
Kinder, Helen Mary	1865	7, 156
Knatchbull, John (Capt.)	1844	314
Knorr, Frances	1893	97v. 2
Lawson, Leonard Keith	1962	263
Lee, Jean	1950	116
Leonski, Edward Joseph	1942	166
Lester, Alfred	1872	97v. 1
McDermott, Frederick Lincoln	1947	66, 166
MacDonald, William	1963	166, 263
Makin (Mr. & Mrs.)	1892	97v. 2
Morris, William Charles	1871	156
Mount, Henry Clarke	1871	156
Nichols, George Robert	1872	97v. 1

MURDER (cont.)
    Palmer, George Charles

Frederick	1859	97v. 1
Ross, Colin Campbell	1922	116, 166
Rowles, Snowy <u>see</u>		
Smith, John Thomas		
Smith, John Thomas		
(alias Rowles)	1932	66
Supple, Gerald Henry	1870	156
Treffene, Phillip John	1926	66
Velonias, Stefanos	1964	263
Willgoss, Walter William	1959	66
Williams, Edward	1924	116
Williams, John "Old Jack"	1859	97v. 1
Wilson, James	1917	97v. 1

Austria

Bauer, Gustav	1930	117
Hofrichter, Adolf	1909	117
Pineau, Henri	1876	259

Bahamas

De Marigny, Alfred (Count)	1943	42, 149, 282

Belgium

Joniaux (Mme.)	1895	309
Peltzer, Leon	c. 1915	123
Risk Allah, Habeeb	1866	276

Canada

Ayalik, Jimmy	1960	168
Bennett, George	1880	127
Birchall, John Reginald	1890	184, 298
Brown, James	1861	127, 298
Bunce, Johnny	c. 1930	20
Carroll, James, et al.	1880-81	127, 298
Delorme, Adelard (Abbé)	1922-24	298
Dick, Evelyn	1946	168
Elliott, Robert J.	1931	20
Ford, Clara	1894	298
Ford, Wayne	1967	168
Gastle, Gordon	1931	20
Gray, Thomas & Hessie	1894	298
Green, George	1850	127
Guay, Joseph Albert	1949-50	217
Hyams, Dallas Theodore		
& Harry Place	1895	127, 298
King, William Henry (Dr.)	1858	298
Larocque, William J.	1932	20
Lavictoire, Emmanuel	1932	20

Lucas, Arthur	1962	168
Nelson, Earle	1927	86
Osborne, John, et al.	1877-78	298
Petri, Marie	1949-50	217
Pratt, Wilton (Dr.)	1934	20
Ruest, Genereux	1949-50	217
Sherrick, John	1861	127, 298
Townsend, William	1857-58	127, 298
Truscott, Steven	1959	11
Turpin, Ronald	1962	168
Ward, Jane	1861	127, 298
Whelan, Patrick James	1868	127, 211, 298
Channel Islands		
De la Mare, E. G. (Mrs.)	1935	253
France		
Algarron, Jacques	1955	109
Avril, Robert	1958	101v. 5
Baillet	1891	18
Bastide, Louis, et al.	1817	120
Bastien	1833	34, 279
Beauvallon, Rosamond de	1846	121
Benoit, Frédéric	1831	118
Berland, Adolphe, et al.	1891	18
Bernardy de Sigoyer	1946	167
Besnard, Marie	1952	252, 292
Bompard, Gabrielle	1890	153, 207, 254
Bonaparte, Pierre Na-		
poléon (Prince)	1870	209
Bouvier, Léone	1953	109
Bower, Elliott	1852	179, 230
Boyer, Marie	1877	153
Breton (Maj.)	1891	18
Brinvilliers: Marquise		
de Brinvilliers see		
D'Aubray, Marie Mar-		
guerite (Marquise de		
Brinvilliers)		
Bruneau, Albert (Abbé)	1892	274
Caillaux, Henriette	1914	11, 117, 167, 292
Calas, Jean	1761	261
Castaing, Edme (Dr.)	1823	153
Cauvin, Louis	1892	309
Chevallier, Yvonne Rous-		
seau	1952	109, 252
Corday, Charlotte	1793	89v. 1, 293
Cournou, Etienne, et al.	1891	18

MURDER (cont.)

D'Aubray, Marie Marguerite (Marquise de Brinvilliers)	1676	37, 86, 180
Dawes, Sophie	1832	120, 273
De Bernardi, Alain	1946	252
Deluzy-Desportes, Henriette	1847	238
De Molen, Roger (Count)	1887	18
Derues, Antoine François	1776	153
De Salis, Jean Baptiste, et al.	1712	279
Dominici, Gaston	1955	101v. 2, 114, 150, 252
Druaux, Pauline	1887	118
Dubisson, Pauline	1951	109, 252
Dumollard, Martin & Marianne	1862	34, 279
Dutilleul	1891	18
Eyraud, Michel	1890	153, 187, 207, 254
Fenayrou, Marion & Gabrielle	1882	153
Feuchères, Sophie de see Dawes, Sophie		
Gelfand, Michel	1953	109
Hilaire, Marcel	1953	109
Jagado, Helène	1851	309
Labbé, Denise	1955	109
Lafarge, Marie	c. 1840	309
Landru, Henri Désiré	1921	2, 7, 37, 86, 148, 149, 161, 189, 195, 266v. 1, 294
Lesnier	c. 1847	118
Lespagne	c. 1847	118
Lesurques, Joseph	1796	65, 154
Mandrin, Louis	1755	99
Meunier (Custom-House Officer)	1891	18
Michel, Marie	1892	309
Orsini, Felice, et al.	1858	159, 266v. 1
Petiot, Marcel (Dr.)	1946	167, 217, 252, 254, 266v. 1
Peytel, Sebastian	1839	120
Pivardière, Louis Charles de la	1698	118, 279

Pranzini, Karl	1887	187
Praslin: Duke of Praslin see Theobald, Charles Laure Hugues (Duke of Praslin)		
Quérangel Family	1881-82	159
Ravaillac, Francis	1610	44v. 1
Robert	1833	34, 279
Sarret, Georges	1933	307v. 1
Seznec, Guillaume	1924	120
Soursas, Simone	1955	109
Steinheil, Marguerite	1909	117
Theobald, Charles Laure Hugues (Duke of Praslin)	1847	52, 89v. 1, 238, 279
Troppmann, Jean Baptiste	1870	86, 209
Vacher, Joseph	1898	167
Vancrose, Fernand de	1898	120
Verger, Jean-Louis	1857	167
Vitalis, Marie	1877	153
Weidmann, Eugen	1939	158
Germany		
Antonini, Joseph, et al.	1809	95
Bichel, Andrew	1808	95
Forster, John Paul	1820	95
Forster, Philip	1820	52
Frisch, Caspar	1809	95, 211
Grupen, Peter	1921	117
Haarmann, Fritz	1924	86, 254
Hau, Karl	1906	117
Holzinger, John Conrad	1819	95
Kleinschrot, Conrad, et al.	1821-22	95, 211
Linsell, Gordon Kenneth	1950	38
Muller, Richard (Dr.)	1954	150
Neumann, Diedrich	1877	35
Rauschmaier, George	1822	95, 211
Riembauer, Francis Salis	1813	95, 211
Schmidt, Abraham	1817	95
Schönleben, Anna	1810	95, 211
Sörgel, John George	1824	95
Steiner, Ludwig	1821	95
Wachs, George	1819	95
Wagner, John Adam	1821-22	211
Zwanziger, Anna see Schönleben, Anna		
Greece		
Mariam (Mother Superior)	1953	252

MURDER (cont.)
  Hungary
    Matuska, Sylvester   1932   117
  India
    Ahmed, Shafi, et al.   1925   4, 105, 262
    Aiyangar, Ramanujam   1934   4
    Apte, Narayan D. , et al.   1948-49   75
    Bawla--Abdul Bawla Mur-
       der see Ahmed,
       Shafi, et al.
    Bhattacharjee, Taranath
       (Dr.)   1934   4
    Clark, Henry (Dr.)   1913   4, 105, 110, 262
    Fulham, Agatha   1913   4, 105, 110, 262
    Godse, Nathuram V. ,
       et al.   1948-49   75, 169
    Hakim Khan Murder   1932   169
    Kadambur   1919   4
    Kaur, Palvinder   1951   169
    Kaur, Rani Bhagwan   1911   105
    Khan, Mohammed Nawaz   1942   105
    Kihsori Case   1948-49   106
    Kishori, Mumtaz   1949   103
    Lagu, Anant Chintaman
       (Dr.)   1958   107
    Laksmikantham Murder
       Case   1944   4
    Mohun, Hurree   1890   105
    Mukerian Dacoity   1957   169
    Mul Raj, Diwan   1849   105
    Nanavati (Com.)   1959-60   105
    Nawaz, Mohammed   1941   4
    Pandes' Trial   1928   4
    Pandey, Benoyendra   1934   4, 105, 262
    Partapendra, Benoyendra   1934-35   75
    Rahim, Abdul   1943-46   103, 106
    Rahmani, Shamim   1969   107
    Ray, Nirmal Kanta   1914   262
    Rura, et al. see Muke-
       rian Dacoity
    Seth, Chandrakant   1956   63
    Singh, Amrik   1948   103, 106, 169
    Singh, Bhagat, et al   1930   104, 262
    Singh, Dharamvir   1957   169
    Singh, Gurbakhsh, et al.   1957-58   169
    Singh, Kartar, et al.   1954   169

Singh, Maharaja Bhupendra   1929   105
Sobani, Begum Omar   1926   107
Taranath (Dr.)   1934   4, 105, 262
Ireland
  Ball, Edward   1936   77
  Cadden, Mary Annie
    "Mamie"   1956   76
  Cross, Philip (Dr.)   1887   88, 315
  Dunne, Patrick   1832   205
  Fleming, John   1933   76
  Gorman, Edward   1924   76
  Gorman, William   1828   89v. 1
  Ireland's Eye Case   see
    Kirwan, William Burke
  Kelly, Edward   1924   76
  Kelly, Thomas   1936   76
  King, Robert (2nd Earl
    of Kingston)   1798   51, 275
  Kingston: 2nd Earl of
    Kingston see King,
    Robert (2nd Earl of
    Kingston)
  Kirwan, Bernard   1943   77
  Kirwan, William Burke   1852-53   43, 179, 230, 238,
                                         241, 242, 250,
                                         259
  Lehman, James H.   1944-45   77
  Malahide Mystery see
    McCabe, Henry
  McCabe, Henry   1926   77
  O'Brien, Jane   1932   77
  O'Leary, Cornelius &
    Hannah   1925   76
  O'Shea, David   1931   76
  O'Shea, William   1943   77
  Pine, Edmond see
    Savage, Daniel
  Savage, Daniel   c. 1835   119
  Scanlan, John   1820   120
  Toal, Gerard   1928   76
Italy
  Montesi Scandal   1954   292
  Nicolaievna, Maria (Count-
    ess Tarnowska)   1910   83
  Tarnowska: Countess
    Tarnowska see

MURDER (cont.)
  Nicolaievna, Maria
  (Countess Tarnowska)
 Kenya
  Bray, George James (Sgt.) 1949 274
  Broughton, Sir Henry
   John Delves 1941 282
  Poole, Peter 1959-60 101v. 7
  Taraoithio Gate wa Baragu 1945-46 274
 Monaco
  Goold, Vere & Marie 83
 New Zealand
  Bayly, William Alfred 1934 7, 254
  Burgess, Richard 1866 289
  Butler, Robert 1880 153, 289
  Cedeno, Simon 1871 289
  Chemis, Louis 1889 289
  Clements, Charles 1897 289
  Coats, George Errol 1931 289
  Collins, James 1861 289
  Cooper, Daniel Richard 1923 289
  Dyer 1874 289
  Eppwright, Joseph 1873 289
  Fisher, William 1873 289
  Flanagan, Anna & Sarah 1891 289
  Good, William 1850 289
  Gunn, Dennis 1920 289
  Hall, Thomas 1886 289
  Houston, Margaret 1886 289
  Hulme, Janet 1954 101v. 2, 116, 254,
        266v. 2, 294
  Kelly, Thomas 1866 289
  Maroro 1849 289
  Parker, Pauline 1954 101v. 2, 116, 254,
        266v. 2, 294
  Phillpot, Frank 1898 289
  Rottman, Arthur 1915 289
  Sullivan, Joseph Thomas 1866 289
  Terry, Lionel 1905 289
  Thorne, Samuel John 1920 289
  Topi, Rutene 1922 289
  Tuhiata 1880 289
  Whakamau 1868 289
  Wilson, James 1867 289
 Poland
  Mazurkiewicz, Wladyslaw 1959 150

Sicily
    Guiliano Gang Trial   1952   252
Singapore
    Hicks, Lutien Roy   1960   101v. 6
South Africa

Name	Year	Page(s)
Bagg, Arthur Richard	1938	29
Blyth, Irene Adelaide	1940	23
Brand, Elizabeth & Maria	1932	30, 48v. 2
Burke, Kenneth Kenwyn	1955	32
Carr, Albert George	1948	23
Chigango, et al.	1923	81
Coetzee, Jacobus Hendrik	1935	25, 29
Coupar, Robert Martin	1906	31
Cox, Frederick William	1924	29
De Beer, Petrus Cornelius	1926	29
De Leeuw, Huibrecht Jacob	1927	24, 30
De Melker, Daisy Louisa	1932	26, 30
Dorosier, Job		81
Du Plessis, Andries Stephanus	1937	25, 29
Du Plessis, Dirkie Cathrina	1926	25, 29
Du Randt, Ian	1953	22, 32
Du Toit, Maria	c. 1930	22
Du Toit, Petrus Hendrik	1932	30
Fisher, Hubert William	1920	31
Gordon-Lennox, Ellen	1923	29
Groesbeek, Maria	1969	28
Grubuxa, Mike	1974	28
Hauptfleisch, Petrus Stephanus François	1925	25, 29
Hodgson, James William	1938	23
Hopewell, John Henry	1938	28
Jackson, Idonie Rubidge	1953	22
Jekhels, Kasper	1890	81
Jones, Bart Stephanus	1888	81
Kerr, Thomas Andrew	1907	22, 32
Knott, Hester Elizabeth	1926	30
Lamprecht, Gert du Plessis	1955	32
Laubscher, Miemie	1957	27
Lee, Maria	1948	29
Liebman, Hyman Balfour	1949	24
Lineveldt, Gamat Salie	1941	23, 28
Lotz, Nicholas Johannes	1955	32
Maclean, Ronald (Maj.)	1910	31

MURDER (cont.)

Mallalien, Richard Louis	1932	26, 30
Markus, Edward William	1926	24, 25
Mathibe, Jacob	1910	81
McDonald, John Edward	1926	29
McLoughlin, Jack	1909	32, 81
Meyer, Claude Toto	1974	28
Moodie, Duncan Donald	1961	27
Morton, Robert	1973	28
Munnik, Jan Willem Hendrik	1932	24, 30
Nel, Dietrich Johannes Willem	1934	31
Nelson, John Henry	1918	31
Nicholls, Albert Raymond Kenneth	1941	31
Nicholson, William Lawrence Warren	1957	28
Nortje, Jan Christian	1926	25, 29
Pattinson, Joseph Colin	1937	27
Polliack, David	1949	24
Rawlinson, William Jackson	1953	22, 32
Rheeder, Margaret Elizabeth	1957	27
Rinaldi, Antonio	1953	22, 32
Roberts, Roland	1957	27
Ross, Charles William	1932	25, 26
Sandwene, Nitmane	1937	24, 25, 28
Smith, Martin Wessels	1950	31
Stanley, Arthur Cromwell (Lt.)	1923	25, 29
Steyh, Hermanus, et al.	1883	81
Swart, Marthinus Erich Walter	1937	31
Swartz, P. J. J.	1903	81
Thomas, Vera	1946	24
Thompson, George	1961	27
Thompson, William, et al.	1838	81
Tolputt, Gwendoline Mary	1932	26, 30
Tshozi, Skelemu	1913	81
Van Breda, Dirk Gysbert	1871	81
Van Breda, Felix Leonard	1958	31
Van Buren, Gordon	1956-57	27
Van der Merwe, Carel Aaron	1837	81

Van der Merwe, Dina		
Dorothea	1921	23
Van Niekerk, Andries		
Petrus	1926	24, 25
Van Rensburg, Barend S.	1923	29
Van Wyk, Stephanus Louis	1930	24, 30, 118
Vermaak, Herbert Vincent	1929	30
Von Veltheim, Franz Lud-		
wig	1898	22, 81
Von Zell, Alfred Percival	1953	22, 32
Wanka, Alfred	1960	27
Westrich, Carl	1927	22
Soviet Union		
De Lacy, Patrick O'Brien	1911	217
Panchenko (Dr.)	1911	217
Sri Lanka		
Dias, Gilbert	1950	5v. 2
Jayewardene, Lenduwa		
Lokuge	1948	5v. 2
Kotalawala, John	1907	5v. 1
Martin, Halpe, et al.	1948-49	5v. 2
Perera, Singhone	1907	5v. 1
Seneviratne, Stephen	1933-36	5v. 1
Singho, Baron	1907	5v. 1
Sugathadasa, Punchihe-		
wage	1957	5v. 1
Velaithan	1941-42	5v. 1
Weerasamy	1941-42	5v. 1
Wijeydasa Perera, Maka-		
witage, et al.	1950	5v. 2
Sweden		
Brekke, Carstein	1949	207
Horsten, Aake, pseud.	1941	227
Kreuger, Alexander	1926	195, 217
Von Arbin, Erik	1926	195, 217
Switzerland		
Hume, Brian Donald	1959	101v. 6, 150
United Kingdom		
Acid-Bath Murderer see		
Haigh, John George		
Adams, John Bodkin (Dr.)	1957	101v. 4, 161
Allaway, Thomas Henry	1922	110, 147, 216, 312
Allen, Margaret	1948	146
Allen, William Philip, et		
al.	1867	43
Aram, Eugene	1759	33, 36, 52, 123, 148
Arden, Alice, et al.	1551	34

MURDER (cont.)
    Ardlamont Mystery see
      Monson, Alfred John
    Armstrong, Herbert
      Rouse (Maj.)   1922   17, 47, 113, 137,
                                                    148, 187, 188,
                                                  232, 259, 285,
                                                  312
    Armstrong, John & Janet   1955   101v. 4
    Arran Murder see Lau-
      rie, John Watson
    Auchindrayne: Lord of
      Auchindrayne see Murc,
      John (Lord of Auchindrayne)
    Azad, Singh   1940   295v. 8
    Badham, George Alexan-
      der   1938   15
    Balham Mystery see
      Cox, Jane Cannon
    Ball, George   1914   78
    Barlow, Kenneth   1957   101v. 5, 255
    Barlow, Silas   1876   49
    Barnes, Peter, et al.   1939   141
    Barney, Elvira Dolores   1932   128, 148, 190, 191,
                                                    228, 253, 259
    Bartlett, Adelaide   1866   7, 108, 120, 123,
                                                    135, 149, 180,
                                                    190, 191, 203,
                                                    206, 238, 241,
                                                    250, 255, 292,
                                                  296
    Bateman, Mary   1809   33, 148
    Bellingham, John   1811   33, 44v. 2, 48v. 2,
                                                    148, 296, 299
    Bennett, Herbert John   1900   157, 184, 207, 282
    Bentley, Derek William   1952   101v. 1, 111, 115,
                                                    157, 218, 220
    Benton, Wallace   1929   147
    Bishop, John   1831   273
    Blandy, Mary   1752   40, 123, 135, 248,
                                                    319
    Branch, Elizabeth & Betty 1740   238, 245
    Bravo, Florence   1876   121, 180, 239, 241,
                                                    250
    Breeds, John   1742   273
    Brennan, Ian   1976-77   21

Brides in the Bath Case
  see Smith, George
  Joseph
Brighton Trunk Murder
  see Mancini, Toni
Brown, Charles Temple-
  man   1946   174
Brown, Ernest   1933   307v. 1
Browne, Frederick Guy   1928   74, 138, 147, 148,
                                          180, 185, 199,
                                          216, 312
Bryant, Charlotte   1936   61, 146, 255
Burke, William   1828   8, 33, 37, 86, 123,
                                          148, 221, 239,
                                          244, 296
Burnett, Kenneth   1974   21
Burnopfield Mystery see
  Cain, John
Burrows, Albert Edward   1923   147
Byrne, Patrick Joseph   1959   101v. 6, 288
Byron, Kittie   1902   17
Byron, William (Lord)   1765   51, 78, 280v. 4
Bywaters, Frederick
  Edward Francis   1922   37, 47, 74, 78, 83,
                                          110, 113, 119,
                                          148, 149, 207,
                                          219, 232
Caddick, Alfred   1952   220
Cain, John   1856   179
Calvert, Louie   1926   146
Camb, James   1948   29, 61, 96, 149,
                                          282, 312
Campbell, Mungo   1770   51
Carr, Robert (Earl of
  Somerset) & Frances
  (Countess of Somerset)   1616   44v. 1, 102, 242
Carraher, Patrick   1938-46   142
Carter, George   1960   101v. 6
Chalkpits Murder see
  Ley, Thomas J.
Chantrelle, Eugène Marie   1878   108
Chaplin, Edward Royal   1938   15
Chapman, George   1903   135
Charing Cross Trunk
  Murder see Robinson,
  John

MURDER (cont.)

Chesney, Donald	1954	101v. 1, 226
Chetwynd, William	1743	314
Christie, John Reginald Halliday	1953	31, 79, 96, 101v. 1, 189, 218, 226, 278, 288, 294
Christofi, Styllou	1954	101v. 2, 146, 266v. 2
Clare, Philip	1857	230
Clark, Joseph Reginald Victor	1928	217
Clark, Violet	1956	101v. 4
Cleft Chin Murder see Jones, Elizabeth Marina & Hulten, Karl Gustav		
Clerk, Duncan	1754	240v. 1, 249, 250
Coleman, Ronald	1953	157
Coningsmark (Count), et al.	1682	280v. 3
Cook, James	1832	186
Corder, William	1828	33, 89v. 1, 148, 211, 296
Cornock, Rosina Ann (Mrs.)	1947	61
Cornwallis, Charles (Lord)	1678	102
Cotton, Mary Ann	1873	179
Courvoisier, François Benjamin	1840	8, 51, 89v. 1, 187, 286v. 1, 296
Cowper, Spencer, et al.	1699	36, 51, 123, 148 280v. 2
Cox, Jane Cannon	1876	121, 180, 239, 241, 250
Coyle, Richard	1741	44v. 2
Craig, Christopher	1952	101v. 1, 111, 115, 157, 218, 220
Cream, Thomas Neill (Dr.)	1892	86, 118, 135, 140, 159, 191, 210, 221, 296, 298, 313
Crippen, Hawley Harvey (Dr.)	1910	47, 74, 90, 94, 124, 136, 143, 148, 207, 210, 221, 232, 255, 266v. 1, 285, 294, 296

Crouch, Harriet Amelia	1926	15
Cunningham, Sawney	1635	211
Dacey, Edwin	1947	220
Daniels, Henry	1960	21
Davies, Michael John	1953	101v. 1, 157
Davy, Flora see Newington, Hannah		
Dearnley, Albert	1923	216
Dhingra, Madar Lal	1909	295v. 8
Diblanc, Marguerite	1872	276
Dickman, John Alexander	1910	41, 123, 185
Dobbs, Hannah	1879	180, 183
Dobkin, Harry	1942	199
Donald, Jeannie	1934	41, 244, 248
Donellan, John (Capt.)	1781	44v. 2, 51, 242
Donovan, George Thomas	1928	173, 216
Dougal, Samuel Herbert	1902	135, 148
Dove, William	1856	49
Dowdall, Michael	1959	288
Drayne, Moses	c. 1662	52
Dudley, Thomas (Capt.), et al.	1884	148, 276
Dunbar, Ronald Patrick	1957	101v. 5
Dunecht Mystery see Soutar, Charles		
Edmonds, Edmund	1872	276
Edmunds, Christina	1871	296, 309
Edward (Earl of Warwick & Holland)	1699	129, 280v. 2
Ellis, Ruth	1955	101v. 3
Ellis, Walter Scott	1961	21
Elltoft, Sam	1914	78
Emmett-Dunne, Frederick (Sgt.)	1955	38, 101v. 3, 254
Emond, Robert	1830	238
Evans, Timothy John	1950	119, 218
Eyre, Edward John	1868	317
Fahmy, Marie-Marguerite	1923	113, 149, 161, 278
Fantle, Ernest	1958	101v. 6
Fenning, Elizabeth	1815	119, 123
Ferrers: 4th Earl of Ferrers see Shirley, Laurence (4th Earl of Ferrers)		
Field, Frederick	1936	282
Field, Herbert Charles	1933	307v. 1

MURDER (cont.)
Field, Jack Alfred	1920	113, 137, 173, 216
Fowler, Henry	1896	132, 180, 216
Fox, Sydney	1930	47, 113, 138, 162, 173, 186, 198, 232, 312
Gale, Sarah	1838	33, 183
Galley, Edmund	1836	70, 118
Gardiner, William	1902-03	180, 185, 273
Gautier, François	1821	245
Giffard, Miles	1953	101v. 1, 157
Gilmour, Christina	1844	240v. 2, 241, 249, 250, 311
Glasgow Cotton Spinners	1838	134
Goodere, Samuel (Capt.), et al.	1741	51, 123, 280v. 2
Gordon, Iain	1953	101v. 1
Gordon, John William	1955	101v. 2
Gorse Hall Murder see Howard, Cornelius		
Goslett, Arthur Andrew	1920	113, 184
Gould, Richard	1840	183
Gray, William Thomas	1920	113, 137, 173, 216
Green, Robert, et al.	1678	36, 44v. 1, 280v. 3
Green Bicycle Mystery see Light, Ronald Vivian		
Greenacre, James	1838	33, 183
Greenwood, David	1918	74, 147
Greenwood, Harold	1920	88, 139, 157, 199, 285
Grondkowski, Marian	1946	61
Gully, James Manby (Dr.)	1876	121, 180, 239, 241, 250
Hackman, James (Rev.)	1779	44v. 2, 51, 314
Hadfield, Albert	1936	15
Haggart, David	1821	123, 247
Haigh, John George	1949	4, 141, 173, 189, 207, 226, 266v. 1 294
Hanratty, James	1962	6, 101v. 7
Hare, William	1828	8, 33, 37, 86, 123, 221, 239, 244, 296
Harries, Ronald	1953	101v. 2, 157, 253
Harrison, Henry	1692	221

Harvey, Sarah	1960	101v. 7
Hayes, Catherine, et al.	1726	33
Hayward, George Frederick Walter	1927	147
Heaman, Peter	1821	245
Hearn, Sarah Ann "Annie"	1931	16, 88, 151, 253
Heath, Neville George Clevely	1946	31, 61, 96, 140, 189, 207, 226, 227, 288, 294, 312
Hepper, William Sanchez de Pina		173
Herbert, Philip (5th Earl of Pembroke)	1678	44v. 1, 51, 73
Heys, Arthur	1945	157
Hinks, Reginald Ivor	1935	158, 253, 307v. 2
Holloway, John William	1831	296
Horne, William Andrew	1759	273
Howard, Cornelius	1909	88, 185
Huggins, John	1729	284v. 2
Hulten, Karl Gustav	1945	149, 312
Hume, Brian Donald	1950	301
Hunt, Joseph	1824	33, 123, 125, 135, 141, 148, 229, 296
Hunter, Thomas	1838	286v. 2
Iggulden, George William	c. 1920	216
Irish Republican Army: I. R. A. Coventry Explosion see Barnes, Peter		
Jackson, William, et al.	1748	280v. 4
Jacoby, Henry	1922	148, 256
Jones, Arthur Albert	1961	101v. 7
Jones, Elizabeth Marina	1945	61, 149, 312
Kehoe, Patrick	1958	220
Keith, Helen Watt	1766	240v. 1, 249
Keith, William	1766	240v. 1, 249
Kello, John (Rev.)	1570	244, 249
Kennedy, Kenneth	1955	101v. 2
Kennedy, William Henry	1928	74, 138, 147, 148, 180, 185, 199, 216, 312
Kennett, Ann	1831	296
Kent, Constance	1860	7, 8, 53, 123, 159, 224, 238, 239,

MURDER (cont.)

		241, 250, 296, 309
Kidd, William (Capt.)	1701	36, 50, 129, 142, 148, 208
Kinloch, Sir Archibald Gordon	1795	319
Kirkwood, James Boyd	1938-39	245
Knowles, Benjamin (Dr.)	1928	282
Königsmark, Charles John (Count), et al.	1682	34, 51, 65, 73, 180
Kowalewski, Czeslaw	1953	220
Lambie, Helen (Witness)	1909	193
Lamson, George Henry (Dr.)	1882	49, 90, 123, 124, 140, 186, 210, 221, 255, 266v.1, 296
Laurie, John Watson	1889	140, 239, 240v. 2, 241, 250
Leany, Daniel	1826	119
Lecky, Dennis Edmond	1943	61
Lee, John	1885	53, 296
Lefroy, Percy see Mapleton, Percy Lefroy		
Le Neve, Ethel	1910	292
Ley, Thomas J.	1947	66, 115, 139, 198, 256, 312
Light, Ronald Vivian	1920	111, 180, 187
Livingston, Jean (Lady Warriston)	1600	249
Loughans, Harold	1944	61
Lowrie, John Watson	1889	249
Luard, Charles Edward (Maj. Gen.)	1908	282, 315
Macdonald, Alexander Bain	1754	240v. 1, 241, 249, 250
Macdonell, Alastair Ronaldson (15th of Glengarry)	1798	243
Mackinnon, Mary	1823	243
MacLeod, Hugh	1831	240v. 1, 241, 247, 250
Macrae, Andrew George	1892	78, 183
Mahon, Patrick Herbert	1924	47, 113, 148, 173, 198, 216, 232

Major, Ethel   1934   146, 255
Malcolm, Sarah   1733   44v. 2
Malinowski, Henryk   1946   61
Manchester Martyrs see
  Allen, William Philip,
  et al.
Mancini, Toni   1934   16, 112, 120, 151,
                                                173, 190, 253,
                                                307v. 2

Manning, George F. &
  Maria   1849   186, 296
Manuel, Peter James
  Anthony   1958   101v. 5, 174, 189
Mapleton, Percy Lefroy   1881   184, 296
Marwood, Ronald Henry   1959   101v. 6
Marymount, Marcus (Sgt.)   1958   101v. 6
Mason, Alexander Camp-
  bell   1923   17, 312
Maybrick, Florence   1889   37, 138, 148, 192,
                                                203, 204, 206,
                                                254, 266v. 2,
                                                285, 309

Maylon, Arthur   1937   15
McLachlan, Jessie   1862   145
McMillan, Margaret   1940   108
McNaughton, Daniel   1843   260
M'Donald, John   1813   245
M'Dougal, Helen   1828   8, 239, 244
Merrett, John Donald   1927   47, 239, 244, 282,
                                                311

Merrett, John Donald see
  also Chesney, Donald
Merrifield, Louisa   1953   101v. 1, 108, 146,
                                                255

Merritt, Ann   1850   49
M'Guigan, John   1935   248, 254
Miao, Chung Y.   1928   120, 147
Mignonette (Ship) Survi-
  vors see Dudley,
  Thomas (Capt.), et al.
Miller, Walter   1870   183
Mills, Herbert Leonard   1951   253
Millsom, Albert   1896   132, 180, 216
M'Kean, James   1796   243
M'Lachlan, Jessie   1862   135, 185, 239, 244,
                                                266v. 2

MURDER (cont.)

M'Naughton, Daniel	1843	163, 286v. 1
Mohon, Charles (Lord)	1692-99	34, 36, 51, 129, 148, 197, 292
Monson, Alfred John	1893	239, 311, 315, 316
Montgomery, Thomas Hartley	1873	43, 319
Moore, Charles	1852	183
Moore, Robert	1953	220
Morrison, Steinie	1911	17, 94, 123, 132, 135, 138, 148, 187, 188, 191, 192, 195, 198, 203, 219, 282, 296
Muller, Franz	1864	186, 296
Mullins, George see Mullins, James		
Mullins, James	1860	53, 183
Murc, John (Lord of Auchindrayne), et al.	1611	247
Murray, William (Maj.)	1861	121
Murtagh, Dennis & Derek	1955	101v. 2
Muschet, Nicol	1720	247
Nairn, Katharine	1765	123, 239, 240v. 1, 249, 319
Newell, Susan	1923	146
Newington, Hannah	1871	276
Nodder, Frederick	1937	141
Norkott, Arthur, et al.	1628	73
Ogilvy, Katharine see Nairn, Katharine		
Ogilvy, Patrick	1765	249
Oliphant, James	1764	243
Onufrejczyk, Michael	1954	101v. 2
Owen, Edgar	1903	186
Ozolins, Vilis	1957	101v. 5
Pace, Beatrice Annie	1928	16, 151
Palmer, William (Dr.)	1856	49, 53, 86, 90, 123, 136, 148, 159, 210, 221, 255, 266v. 1, 294, 296
Parker, Frederick	1934	113, 173
Patch, Richard	1806	275
Payne, Augustus	1887	274

Peace, Charles	1878	37, 153, 187, 229, 259, 296
Peake, Arthur Jefferson	1936	15
Peasenhall Mystery see		
Gardiner, William		
Pelizzioni, Serafino	1866	46, 70, 119, 179
Pembroke: Earl of Pembroke see Herbert, Philip (5th Earl of Pembroke)		
Penge Mystery see Staunton, Louis & Patrick		
Perry, John, et al.	1660	52, 73, 280v. 3
Phillips, John Stanley	1938	15
Pimlico Mystery see Bartlett, Adelaide		
Podmore, William Henry	1930	187
Podola, Guenther Fritz Erwin	1959	101v. 6, 163
Pook, Edmund	1871	185, 276, 292
The Porthole Case see Camb, James		
Prince, Richard Arthur	1898	296
Pritchard, Edward William (Dr.)	1865	8, 49, 90, 124, 139, 145, 210, 239, 241, 250, 255, 296
Probert, Albert	1934	113, 173
Pugh, Joseph, et al.	1828	230
Queen, Peter	1927	174
Rattenbury, Alma	1935	7, 61, 140, 148, 193, 206, 266v. 1, 292, 312
Raven, Daniel	1949	96
Rayne, Richard	1856	179
Read, James Canham	1894	78, 184
Red Barn Murder see Corder, William		
Richardson, Grace	1956	101v. 4
Richardson, John	1737	229
Roberts, Frederick Thomas	1941-42	61
Roberts, George	1953	101v. 1
Robertson, James Ronald	1950	174
Robinson, John	1927	132, 148, 187, 232

MURDER (cont.)

Rouse, Alfred Arthur	1930	16, 47, 128, 135, 142, 148, 151, 198, 219, 232, 253, 266v. 1, 312
Rowland, Walter Graham	1946-47	118, 119, 218
Rumbold, Freda	1956	101v. 4
Rush, James Blomfield	1849	183
Russell, George		157
Russell, Hannah	1826	119
Ruxton, Buck (Dr.)	1936	16, 124, 138, 143, 148, 151, 207, 210, 253, 266v.1, 312
St. Fergus Affair see Smith, William		
Sandyford Mystery see M'Lachlan, Jessie		
Sangret, August	1943	312
Savage, Richard	1727	52
Seaman, William	1896	187
Seddon, Frederick Henry	1912	17, 37, 47, 74, 75, 90, 94, 132, 135, 148, 191, 232, 296, 297
Sheen, William	1827	230
Sheward, William	1869	183, 230, 276
Shirley, Laurence (4th Earl of Ferrers)	1760	33, 44v. 2, 51, 89v. 1, 102, 148, 180, 197, 260, 278
Slater, Oscar	1909-28	42, 46, 83, 111, 119, 123, 136, 143, 145, 193, 239, 244, 266v. 1
Smethurst, Thomas (Dr.)	1859	49, 70, 119, 124, 142, 210, 219, 221
Smith, Alfonso Francis Austin	1926	282
Smith, George Joseph	1915	17, 47, 74, 86, 132, 135, 137, 148, 203, 204, 232, 294, 312

Smith, Jim "Gipsy"	1960	101v. 7
Smith, Lawrence John	1947	66, 115, 139, 198, 312
Smith, Madeleine	1857	8, 37, 49, 123, 134, 136, 143, 145, 148, 180, 193, 224, 239, 254, 266v. 2, 278, 296, 309, 311
Smith, Mary Elder	1827	240v. 2, 249
Smith, William (Dr.)	1854	230, 240v. 2, 244, 248, 249
Somerset: Earl & Countess of Somerset see Carr, Robert (Earl of Somerset) & Frances (Countess of Somerset)		
Stanfield, Annie Amelia	1896	148
Stanfield, Philip	1688	51, 73, 240v. 1, 249
Stanfield Hall Murder see Rush, James Blomfield		
Starchfield, John	1914	185
Staunton, Louis & Patrick	1877	53, 83, 135, 191, 193, 296
Stent, Henry	1819	52
Stewart, James	1753	44v. 2, 135
Stoner, George Percy	1935	7, 61, 140, 148, 193, 206, 266v. 1, 292, 312
Stourton, Charles (Lord)	1557	51, 180, 229
Straffen, John Thomas	1952	142, 163, 256
Strangeways, George (Maj.)	1658	37
Stratton, Albert & Alfred	1905	199
Stuart, James	1822	51, 286v. 1
Tapner, Benjamin, et al.	1749	33
Tawell, John	1845	49
Taylor, Louisa Jane	1882	255, 273
Taylor, Percival Leonard	1928	173, 216
Terry, Victor John	1961	101v. 7
Thompson, Edith Jessie	1922	37, 47, 78, 83, 110, 113, 119, 148, 149, 191, 192, 207, 219, 232, 278
Thorne, Norman	1924	47, 113, 148, 157,

MURDER (cont.)

		162, 173, 186, 191, 192, 232
Thornton, Abraham	1817	44v. 2, 46, 65, 185, 211
Thurtell, John	1824	8, 33, 44v. 2, 123, 125, 135, 141, 148, 186, 229, 296
Toomey, Alexander	1934	245
Townley, George Victor	1863	274, 314
Townshend, Frederick (Lord)	1796	274
True, Ronald	1922	113, 135, 137, 148, 256
Trunk Murders see Mancini, Toni & Robinson, John		
Vaquier, Jean Pierre	1924	113, 128, 148, 216, 232
Voisin, Louis Marie Joseph	1917	17, 94, 216, 232
Waddingham, Dorothea	1936	146, 255
Wainwright, Henry & Thomas	1875	53, 125, 135, 296
Waite, Raymond	1952	220
Wall, Joseph (Gov. of Goree)	1802	40, 48v. 1, 50, 148, 317, 318
Wallace, William Herbert	1931	7, 31, 70, 83, 88, 184, 191, 192, 203, 204, 206, 217, 254, 259, 278
Walters, Rowland, et al.	1688	51
Wardell, William Horsley	c. 1920	216
Warner, Charles	1912	248
Warriston: Lady Warriston see Livingston, Jean (Lady Warriston)		
Warwick: Earl of Warwick & Holland see Edward (Earl of Warwick & Holland)		
Watson, John Selby (Rev.)	1871-72	179, 317
Weaver, James	1928	173, 216

Webster, Kate	1879	123, 187, 206, 266v. 2, 296
West Port Murders see Burke, William & Hare, William		
Weston, Richard	1615	221
Wheeler, Mary Eleanor (alias Mrs. Pearcy)	1890	159
Whelpton, George	1947	220
Whiteway, Alfred Charles	1953	101v. 1, 157, 288
Wilde, Mark	1910	88
Wilkinson, Alec	1955	220
Williams, John	1911	128
Williams, Thomas	1831	273
Wilson, Constance	1862	230
Wilson, Howard, et al.	1970	21
Wilson, Mary Elizabeth	1958	101v. 5
Winslow, Thomas	1860	49
Winsor, Charlotte	1865-66	179
Wood, Robert	1907	88, 110, 112, 132, 139, 157, 180, 184, 190, 191, 259
Wooldridge, Charles Thomas	1896	296
Woolmington, Reginald	1935	61
Yarham, Samuel	1844	185, 230
Yorkshire Witch see Bateman, Mary		
United States		
Abbott, Burton W.	1955	41, 79, 308
Alex, Michael	1931-38	265
Applegate, Everett C.	1936	170
Archer-Gilligan (Mrs.)	1916-19	272
Armstrong, William "Duff"	1858	2, 208
Arnold, Samuel	1865	181v. 8
Arrison, William	1854	181v. 5
Atzerodt, George A.	1865	181v. 8
Avery, Ephraim K. (Rev.)	1833	211, 224
Ballem, Francis Xavier	c. 1956	79
Ballew, Stephen M.	1871	181v. 7
Beauchamp, Jeroboam O.	1826	160
Beck, Martha	1949-51	110, 251
Becker, Charles (Lt.)	1912-14	178, 195
Becker, Max	1930	222

MURDER (cont.)

Berger, Bertha		308
Billik, Herman	1907	272
Billings, Warren	1916	131
Birch, Leroy, et al. see		
Dragon Gang (N. Y.)		
Bjorkland, Diane	c. 1957	79
Black, Crawford	1871	165, 268v. 1-2
Blair, John		54
Blake, Patrick	1816	181v. 1
Bodine, Polly	1844-46	68
Boggie, Clarence Gilmore	1935	42
Boland, Jack "Bobo"	1935	165
Bolton, Mildred	1936	313
Bonds, Jack Whitfield	1963	85
Bonnie, Lola Ida Hemri	1901	165
Boorn, Stephen & Jesse	1819	120, 181v. 6, 211, 225
Borden, Lizzie	1893	11, 161, 178, 186, 191, 192, 223, 224, 225, 257, 292, 294
Boston Massacre Soldiers	1700	62v. 1, 98, 177, 281
Boston Strangler see		
De Salvo, Albert		
Botkin, Cordelia	1898	155, 272
Bowen, George	1816	181v. 1
Bowers, J. Milton (Dr.)	1886-87	272
Brace, Philander	1856	181v. 15
Bram, Thomas Mead		
Chambers	1896-98	187, 225
Brooks, Hugh M.	1886	181v. 13
Brown, Charles T.	1920	60
Brown, E. M. (Dr.)	1863	67
Brown, J. B.	1901	120
Buchalter, Louis "Lepke"	1940	178
Buchanan, Robert W.		
(Dr.)	1893	215, 272
Buckhout, Isaac van Wart	1870-71	67
Buford, Thomas (Col.)	1879	160
Burch, Arthur	1922	234
Burks, Harold Finnon		
"Arkansas"	1941-42	231
Burnham, Josiah	1806	181v. 8
Burns, Florence	1901	215
Burtlett, Mike	1960	165

Caffee, William	1842	80
Campisciano, Ignazio & Maria, et al.	1907	283
Carawan, George W. (Rev.)	1853	181v. 6, 268v. 6
Caritativo, Bart	1955	79
Carnal, Henri	1851	68
Carson, Robert "Sonny"	1973	13
Carter, Kid	1913	196
Caruso, Francesco	1927-28	178
Casey, James P.	1856	181v. 15
Cero, Gongi	1928	196
Chapman, Lucretia	1832	35, 181v. 6, 211, 238
Cherry, Noah, et al.	1873	181v. 3
Cluverius, Thomas J.	1885	181v. 17
Coffey, William N.	1926	80
Cole, George W.	1868	268v. 2
Colson, David (Col.)	1900	160
Colt, John C.	1842	89v. 1, 181v. 1
Coo, Eva	1934	170
Coolidge, Valorus P. (Dr.)	1848	181v. 3, 211
Coough, Joel	1833	181v. 1
Copeland, John Anthony	1859	181v. 6
Coppolino, Carl (Dr.)	1966	12, 41
Cora, Charles	1856	181v. 15
Corey-Price Case	1925	196
Covell, Arthur	1923	42
Crawford, Annie	1911	283
Cream, Thomas Neill (Dr.)	1881	313
Creighton, Mary Frances	1936	170
Crimmins, Alice	1965	277
Croker, Richard	1874	67, 268v. 6
Crowninshield, Richard Jr.	1830	181v. 7
Crump, Paul	1953	212
Cunningham, Emma Augusta	1857	67, 181v. 5, 224
Curtis, Winslow	1826	35
Cvek, George Joseph	1941	231
Czolgosz, Leon F.	1901	181v. 14
Dague, Walter Glenn	1930	126
Davis, Angela	1972	10
Dean, Cyrus B.	1808	181v. 3

MURDER (cont.)

De Graff, William	1912	223
DeMina, Carolino	1832	181v. 6
DeSalvo, Albert	1967	12
Deschamps, Etienne	1889	283
Desha, Isaac B.	1824	160
DeWolf, Orrin	1843	181v. 10
Dockery, John	1893	265
Dooley, Alvin	1940	233, 259
Dragon Gang (N. Y.)	1957	178
Duca, Peter	1928	126
Duker, Herman W.	1931	291
Dunbar, Reuben		268v. 1
Durrant, Henry Theodore	1895	181v. 15, 184, 268v. 1, 295v. 8
Duvall, William Potts	1869	80
Eaton, Gerald	1868	181v. 5
Edgerly, George	1961	12, 257
Edwards, Robert Allen	1934	170
Eidinoff, Harold (Dr.)	1959	85
Elliott, Moses Chapman	1834	211
Engel, George, et al.	1886	181v. 12
Epes, William Dandridge	1848	181v. 3
Esposimina, Lino Amalia	1832	35, 238
Faiman, Charles C. (Dr.)	1925	54
Fair, Laura D.	1871	155, 181v. 15, 209, 265
Farwell, Hartwell	1922	80
Fernandez, Raymond	1949-51	110, 251
Fielden, Samuel. et al.	1886	181v. 12
Finch, Bernard (Dr.)	1961	6, 170
Fiorenza, John	1936	231
Fischer, Adolph, et al.	1886	181v. 12
Fook, Liu	1930	155
The Fox see Hickman, William Edward		
Frank, Leo M.	1913	56, 131, 176, 181v.10
Freeman, William	1846	177, 181v. 16, 268v. 3
Fritz, Ernest	1920	144
Galentine, Jay F. (Dr.)	1871	19
Gallo, Sam	1928	196
German Submariners	1944	304
Gibbs, Edward Lester	1950	178
Gillette, Chester	1906-08	178
Gilman, Ephraim	1862	181v. 7

Graham, Barbara	1953	79
Graham, John Gilbert	1956	251, 278
Graves, Thomas Thatcher		
(Dr.)	1891	181v. 13, 223
Gray, Henry Judd	1927	83, 100v. 2, 178,
		206, 235, 258
Green, Henry G.	1845	181v. 17, 211
Green, Shields	1859	181v. 6
Greenberg, Samuel	1931	222
Gross, Louis	1933-49	42
Grunzig, Otto	1851	68
Guiteau, Charles Julius	1881	149, 165, 181v. 14
Hafner, Bertha	1929	126
Hall, Carl Austin	1953	251
Hall, Frances Stevens	1926	58, 149, 178, 208,
		235, 258
Hall, William	1893	265
Hanion, John	1870	181v. 3
Hardy, William	1806	265
Harris, Carlyle W.	1892	120, 208, 215, 224,
		272
Harris, Mary	1865	165, 181v. 17
Hart, Nathan F.	1878	223
Hartung, Mary	1859	265
Hauer, John, et al.	1798	62v. 2
Hauptmann, Richard Bruno	1935	11, 57, 100v. 1,
		148, 161, 178,
		233, 303
Haymarket Defendants	1886	98, 133, 208, 299
Haymarket Defendants	1893	177
Haywood, William D.	1907	57, 268v. 1
Heady, Bonnie Brown	1953	251
Heirens, William	1946	79, 231
Hendrickson, John	1853	35
Henry, Toni Jo	1941-42	231
Henwood, Frank Harold	1911-14	60
Herbert Fuller (Ship)		
Mystery see Bram,		
Thomas Mead Chambers		
Herold, David E.	1865	181v. 8
Hersey, George C.	1861	211
Hickman, William Edward	1928	217
Hightower, William A.	1921	155
Hoch, Johann	1905-06	272
Hoffman, Harry L.	1929	100v. 2, 120, 144,
		222, 233

MURDER (cont.)

Holman, Jacob	1819	160
Holmes, Herman H.	1895	153, 187, 295v. 8, 298, 313
House, LeRoy & Mrs. House	1941-43	231
How, David D.	1824	181v. 6
Huberman, Gus	1930	234
Hughes, John W. (Dr.)	1865	181v. 2
Hunter, Benjamin F.	1878	181v. 13
Hurd, Roosevelt Carlos (Sr.), et al.	1947	301
Hyde, Bennett Clark (Dr.)	1910-11	272
Icardi, Aldo (Lt.)	1956	269
Industrial Workers of the World (IWW)	1917	144
IWW	1920	131
Ingersoll, Sarah	1873	80
Irwin, Robert	1938	233
Israel, Harold	1924	42, 177
James, Frank	1883	181v. 11, 235
James, Robert S. see Lisenba, Major Raymond		
Jayne, Silas	1971	13
Jefferds, Charles	1861	72
Johnson, Alex	1912	268v. 5
Johnson, Allen	1960	165
Johnson, Edward T. (Capt.)	1884	268v. 8
Johnson, John	1824	181v. 2
Johnson, John A. "Dog-skin"	1911	80
Jordan, Chester S.	1909	196
Joyce, John	1808	181v. 7
Joyce, Johnny	1920	19
Judd, Winnie Ruth	1932	231, 234
Keller, Edward	1916	184
Kelly, John R.	1871	181v. 4
Kennedy, Samuel J. (Dr.)	1899-1901	72, 215
Kinney, Hannah	1840	181v. 17
Knapp, John Francis & Joseph Jenkins	1830	181v. 7, 211, 224, 268v. 2
Lafon, Thomas, Jr.	1869	181v. 4
Lamson, David	1933	118, 179
Latimer, Irving	1889	122
LeDoux, Emma	1906-10	155

Leopold, Nathan: Leopold & Loeb	1924	57, 79, 100v. 2, 149, 178, 195, 235, 294, 303
Leyra, Camilo Weston	1950	178
Lingg, Louis, et al.	1886	181v. 12
Lisenba, Major Raymond	1936	178, 217, 234
Loeb, Richard A. see Leopold, Nathan: Leopold & Loeb		
Long, Kenneth R.	1948	144, 308
Loomis, Frank (Dr.)	1927	122
Lowell, Jim	1874	35
Lowenberg, Moses	1861-63	68
Lusk, Grace	1917	80, 181v. 14
Lyddane, Anne	1935	165
Lyles, Anjette	1958	41
Lyons, Lewis W.	1903	283
Macfarland, Daniel	1870	35, 179
Macfarland, William Allison	1912	272
Magnuson, John	1923	80
Manson, Charles	1971	161
Manster, Harry	1918	196
Marchant, Charles	1826	35
Mark & Phillis (Negro Slaves)	1755	181v. 11
Martin, Hymie	1931	19
Mayberry, David F.	1855	181v. 2
Mazzerella, Vincenzo	1922	126
McClellan, Fred Athens	1924	202
McConaghy, Robert	1840	181v. 10
McGannon, William H. (Judge)	1920	19
McGowan, Edward	1857	181v. 15
McLeod, Alexander	1841	181v. 7
McLucas, Lonnie	1969	277
McManus, George C.	1929	258
Meyer, Henry C. (Dr.)	1893	215
Mikulicz, Joseph	1950	277
Mitchell, Steve	1950	85
Molineaux, Roland Burnham	1899-1900	149, 215, 224, 272
Monahan, Annie F.	1917-19	272
Mooney, Thomas J.	1916	131, 176
Morey, William	1951	157

MURDER (cont.)

Mossler, Candace "Candy"	1966	85
Motherwell, Larry Lord	1960	165
Mudd, Samuel A. (Dr.)	1865	181v. 8
Murdaugh, John	1839	160
National Textile Workers Union (Gastonia, N.C.)	1929	131
Neagle, David	1889	181v. 15, 287
Neebe, Oscar W., et al.	1886	181v. 12
Neu, Kenneth	1933	283
Newton, Huey P.	1968	39
Nolan, Charles	1880	80
Noxon, John F.	1944	178
Obenchain, Madalynne	1922	234
O'Laughlin, Michael	1865	181v. 8
O'Loughlin, Pearl	1930	60
Orpet, William	1916	120, 272, 313
Panther Torture Case see McLucas, Lonnie		
Parr, Laura	1935	233
Patrick, Albert T.	1900	295v. 2
Patrick, Albert T.	1902	58, 215, 223, 295v. 2
Patterson, Gertrude Gibson	1911	60
Patterson, Nan	1904-05	178
Peete, Louise	1944	79, 234
Pell, Max	1951	157
Peltz, Greta	1936	170
Perry, Arthur	1937	72, 157
Peyton, Charles	1948	126
Phillips, Billy	1972	13
Phillips, Clara	1922	234
Pizzino, Ted, et al.	1930	122
Pope, Ervin	1909	118
Powers, Caleb, et al.	1900-06	58, 160
Prescott, Abraham	1834	181v. 5
Prior, Tab, et al.	1893	80
Probst, Anton	1866	268v. 4
Puglise, James	1922	126
Purvis, Will	1893	118
Radcliffe, William	1852	80
Rattlesnake Murder see Lisenba, Major Raymond		
Ray, James Earl	1968	85, 267, 303
Redenbaugh, Joseph	c. 1917	227

Reilly, James A. (D. A.), et al.	1936	126
Richeson, Clarence V. T.	1911	272
Robbins, Jonathan	1799	181v. 7, 302
Robinson, Cecil John	1958	41
Robinson, Henrietta	1854	35, 181v. 11
Robinson, Richard P.	1836	89v. 1, 181v. 12, 211
Rodriguez, Roman	1952	79
Rogers, Silas	1943	42
Rubenstein, Pasach N.	1876	268v. 4
Ruby, Jack	1964	269
Rulloff, Edward H.	1871	265
Russ, Calvin	1847	68
Rutledge, Robert C. (Dr.)	1949	231
Sacco, Nicola: Sacco & Vanzetti	1921-27	2, 10, 11, 57, 100v. 1, 130, 148, 149, 176, 177, 235, 271, 281, 293, 303
Sander, Hermann (Dr.)	1950	251
Schroeder, Irene	1930	126
Schwab, Michael, et al.	1886	181v. 12
Schwartz, Harry	1887	313
Schweitzer, William, et al.	1935	122
Scott, Leonard Ewing	1957	41
Seale, Bobby G.	1970	39, 290
Selfridge, Thomas O.	1806	181v. 2
Sellick, Diana	1816	181v. 2
Shay, Mortimer	1860	68
Shepherd, William	1925	54
Sheppard, Samuel (Dr.)	1954	12, 170, 178, 251
Sickles, Daniel E.	1859	34, 35, 181v. 12, 165, 208, 268v. 7, 281
Simpson, Ann K.	1850	181v. 5, 268v. 6
Sirhan, Sirhan Bishara	1969	267, 303
Small, Frederick L.	1917	217, 223
Smith, Christian	1817	181v. 1
Smith, Richard	1816	181v. 5
Snook, James Howard (Dr.)	1929	231
Snyder, Ruth	1927	83, 100v. 2, 178, 206, 235, 258

MURDER (cont.)

Southard, Elizabeth	1851	181v. 2
Spangler, Edward	1865	181v. 8
Spencer, Eliphalet M. S.	1846	68
Spies, August, et al. see Haymarket Defendants		
Spooner, Bathsheba	1778	62v. 2, 181v. 2, 208
Stein, Harry	1931	222
Stengel, Otto, et al. see German Submariners		
Stephenson, David C.	1925	56, 178
Stevens, Henry & William	1926	149, 178, 208, 235, 258
Stielow, Charles F.	1915	42
Strunk, Ira	1886	268v. 5
Suratt, John H.	1867	181v. 9
Sweet, Ossian H. (Dr.), et al.	1925-27	98, 130
Sykes, Troisville	1884	283
Talle, Tom	1950	308
Tenants Harbor (Maine) Mystery see Hart, Nathan F.		
Terry, David S. (Judge)	1856	181v. 15
Thacker, William J.	1901	265
Thaw, Harry	1907	83, 100v. 1, 111, 268v. 1, 235
Thayer, Israel, Jr., & Isaac & Nelson	1825	181v. 7
Thompson, Louis	1947	122
Thompson, Phil B., Jr.	1883	160
Thompson, Phil B., Sr., et al.	1873	160
Thomson, Samuel	1809	181v. 11
Tirrell, Albert J.	1846	196, 211
Tregoff, Carole	1961	6, 170
Trunk Murder see Judd, Winnie Ruth		
Tse-ne-gat	1915	60
Tucker, Charles Louis	1905	225
Tulley, Samuel	1812	181v. 1
Turco, Arthur	1971	277
Twitchell, George S.	1868	181v. 6
Udderzook, William E.	1873	224
Vanzetti, Bartolomeo see Sacco, Nicola: Sacco & Vanzetti		

Vermilya, Louise	1912	272
Vineyard, James R.	1842	80
Wagner, Louis	1873	224
Waite, Arthur Warren (Dr.)	1916	272
Walburger, Dotty	1930	234
Waldo, Deloris	1948	126
Wan, Ziang Sun	1920-26	165, 202
Ward, John	1866	181v. 14
Ward, Matthews F.	1854	160, 181v. 3
Ward, Thomas	1823	181v. 4
Waring, John U.	1835	160
Watt, Newton	1887	313
Webb, Madeline, et al.	1942	231
Webster, John White (Dr.)	1850	37, 123, 153, 178, 181v. 4, 208, 211, 224, 235
Weeks, Levi	1800	181v. 1
Weems, William, et al.	1770	181v. 10
Wentzel, George C.	1946	42
Wharton, Elizabeth G.	1871-72	165, 209
Wheeler, Mary Ann	1842	80
Whitfield, John Leonard	1923	19
Wilkins, Walter Keene (Dr.)	1919	72
Wilkinson, Benjamin R. (Dr.)	1839	160
Wilkinson, Edward C. (Judge)	1839	160, 181v. 1, 268v. 1-2
William Brown (Sailing Ship)	1842	268v. 3, 287
Williams, John	1921	281
Willner, Josephine	1876	80
Wirz, Henry (Capt.)	1865	181v. 8
The Wobblies see Industrial Workers of the World (IWW)		
Wolcott, Harold	1933	158
Worrell, Edward D.	1857	181v. 10
Wynekoop, Alice (Dr.)	1933	313
Youtsey, Henry, et al.	1900	160
Zoldoske, Rose	1891	80

MURDER (ATTEMPTED MURDER)
   Australia
      Dean, George   1895   69, 156
      Dowell, Kerry Ronald   1967   263
      Kocan, Peter   c. 1965   263
   France
      Baffier, Jean   1887   18
      Delgove (Justice of the
        Peace)   1887   18
      Demon, Henri   1951   109
      Gontaut, Gabriel   1887   18
   India
      Gaekwar, Mulhar Rao 1875   214
   Ireland
      Delany, John   1832   205
      Nash, Patrick   1822   205
   United Kingdom
      Brudenell, James Thomas
        (Earl of Cardigan)   1841   51, 65, 102, 148,
                                      197, 230, 286v. 1,
                                      317, 318
      Cardigan, Earl of _see_
        Brudenell, James
        Thomas (Earl of Cardigan)
      Chicago May _see_ Church-
        ill, May Vivienne
      Churchill, May Vivienne 1907   17
      Coke, Arundel   1722   52, 274
      Saunders, John   1913   245
      Smith, Charles   1907   17
      Wheeler, Mavis   1954   101v. 2
   United States
      Black Panthers (Chicago) 1970   39
      Bursey, Charles   1969   39
      Hagerman, Henry B.   1818   181v. 14
      Lawrence, Richard   1835   181v. 3
      Northrop (White Plains,
        N. Y. Case)   1866   68
      Schenck, John O. (Mrs.) 1911   272
      Wells, Warren   1969   39

MUTINY
   United Kingdom
      Bounty (Ship) Mutineers
        see Heywood, Peter,
        et al.

Heywood, Peter, et al.	1792	50, 148
Johnston, George (Maj.)	1811	275
Parker, Richard, et al.	1797	38, 44v. 2, 50
United States		
Amistad (Schooner)	1840	98, 287

NEGLIGENCE
United Kingdom
Tay Bridge Disaster En-
| quiry | 1880 | 134 |
Titanic (Ship) Investiga-
| tion | 1912 | 297, 299 |
United States
Adams, Richard
Adams v. Miami-Dade
| County Jail | 1968 | 236 |
Andrea Doria/Stockholm
Ricolo v. Andrea Doria/
| Stockholm | 1957-59 | 9 |
Been, Hyman
Been v. Sears, Roe-
| buck & Co. | 1968 | 236 |
Burgel, Gus
Burgel v. Red Wing
| Carriers | 1968 | 236 |
Cutter Laboratories
Gottsdanker & Phipps
| v. Cutter Laboratories | 1957 | 9, 257 |
DeVito, Mary
DeVito v. United Air-
lines Co. & Douglas Air-
| craft Co. | 1951 | 9 |
Dillon, Arthur
Dillon v. Miami-Dade
| County | 1973 | 236 |
Donelon, John Joseph
(Mrs.)
Donelon v. Long Island
| Railroad | 1951 | 213 |
Douglas Aircraft Co.
DeVito v. United Air-
lines Co. & Douglas
| Aircraft Co. | 1951 | 9 |
Eastland (Ship) Investiga-
| tion | 1915 | 299 |

NEGLIGENCE (cont.)
    Edwards, Carmen
      Edwards v. Missouri-
      Kansas-Texas Railroad
      Co. , et al.   1957   9
    Gillespie, John Birks
      "Dizzy"
      Gillespie v. Nachbar   9
    Gottsdanker, Josephine
      Gottsdanker & Phipps
      v. Cutter Laboratories   1957   9, 257
    Laidlaw, William R.
      Laidlaw v. Sage   1892-95 295v. 7
    Long Island Railroad
      Donelon v. Long Island
      Railroad   1951   213
    Miami Beach (City)
      Vega v. City of Miami
      Beach   1973   236
    Miami-Dade County
      Dillon v. Miami-Dade
      County   1973   236
    Miami-Dade County Jail
      Adams v. Miami-Dade
      County Jail   1968   236
      Robinson v. Miami-
      Dade County Jail   1970   236
    Miami-Dade County Sheriff
      Williams v. Miami-Dade
      County Sheriff   1969   236
    Missouri-Kansas-Texas
      Railroad Co. , et al.
      Edwards v. Missouri-
      Kansas-Texas Railroad
      Co. , et al.   1957   9
    Nachbar, Joachim
      Gillespie v. Nachbar   9
    Red Wing Carriers
      Burgel v. Red Wing
      Carriers   1968   236
    Ricolo, Angela
      Ricolo v. Andrea Doria/
      Stockholm   1957-59 9
    Robinson, Michael
      Robinson v. Miami-Dade
      County Jail   1970   236

Sage, Russell
   Laidlaw v. Sage   1892-95   295v. 7
Sears, Roebuck & Co.
   Been v. Sears, Roe-
     buck & Co.   1968   236
Titanic (Ship) Investiga-
   tion   1912   299
United Airlines Co.
   DeVito v. United Air-
   lines Co. & Douglas
   Aircraft Co.   1951   9
Vega, Nobel
   Vega v. City of Miami
   Beach   1973   236
Vestris (Ship) Investiga-
   tion   1929-32   295v. 6
Williams, Johnnie Lee
   Williams v. Miami-
   Dade County Sheriff   1969   236

NEUTRALITY (BREACH OF
NEUTRALITY)
   Switzerland
     Alabama Arbitration
      United States v. Gt.
      Brit.   1872   133
   United States
     Guinet, John Etienne   1795   181v. 4, 302
     Henfield, Gideon   1793   181v. 4, 302
     Meteor (Steamship)   1866   209
     Williams, Isaac   1799   181v. 12

OBSCENITY
   Canada
     African Ballet   1967   168
     Fanny Hill (Novel)   1964   168
   United Kingdom
     Ellis, Havelock, et al.   1897   59
     Lady Chatterley's Lover
     (Novel)   1960   101v. 7
   United States
     American Mercury (Bos-
     ton)   1926-27   130
     The Captive (Drama)   1927   130

OBSCENITY (cont.)
    Fanny Hill (Novel)   1964   257
    Hazeltine, Charles   1873   181v. 11

PANDERING
    India
        Krishna, Hare   1937   262
    United Kingdom
        Jeffries, Mary (Mrs.)   1887   228
        Messina, Alfredo   1951   150
        Morriss, Hayley   1925   15
        Profumo Affair see
          Ward, Steven (Dr.)
        Ward, Steven (Dr.)   1963   228
    United States
        Jelke, Mickey   1953   150
        Wittenburgh, Francis   1818   181v. 1

PERJURY
    United Kingdom
        Canning, Elizabeth   1754   65, 260
        Castro, Thomas see
          Orton, Arthur
        Druce, Herbert   1901-08 216
        Oates, Titus   1685   221
        Orton, Arthur   1873   8, 94, 209, 260,
                                      287, 295v. 3
    United States
        Carroll, Earl   1926   295v. 7
        Hiss, Alger   1949   56, 100v. 2, 176,
                                        208, 257
        Hummel, Abe   1905   195
        Lehman, Julius   1902   181v. 9

PIRACY
    United Kingdom
        Green, Thomas (Capt.),
          et al.   1705   247
        Kidd, William (Capt.)   1701   36, 50, 129, 142,
                                      148, 208
    United States
        Bird, Thomas   1790   181v. 14
        Bonnet, Stede "Major",
          et al.   1718   181v. 4

Brierly, John, et al.   1718   181v. 4
Gilbert, Pedro, et al.   1834   181v. 10
Hansen, Hans   181v. 14
Hicks, Albert   1860   181v. 14
Quelch, John (Capt.),
    et al.   1704   181v. 5
Trucker, Robert, et al.   1718   181v. 4

PLAGIARISM
  United States
    Baron, Maurice
      Baron v. Leo Feist,
      Inc.   1947   213
    Leo Feist, Inc.
      Baron v. Leo Feist,
      Inc.   1947   213
    Rum and Coca-Cola (Song)
      see Leo Feist, Inc.

POLICE BRUTALITY
  United States
    Hallinan, Terence
      Hallinan v. Brady,
      County of San Francisco,
      and Gutierrez   1973   269
    San Francisco County
      Hallinan v. Brady,
      County of San Francisco,
      and Gutierrez   1973   269

PROHIBITION (WRIT)
  United States
    Hall, A. Oakey (Mayor of
      N. Y.), et al.   1871   67

PROSTITUTION
  United Kingdom
    Cass, Elizabeth   1887   46

RAPE
  Australia
    Buttner, Ernest   1889   69

RAPE (cont.)

Mount Rennie Case	1886	69
India		
Mahesh	1960	107
United Kingdom		
Baltimore: Lord Balti- more see Calvert, Frederick (Baron of Baltimore)		
Calvert, Frederick (Baron of Baltimore)	1768	275
Cant, George	1839	70
United States		
Chessman, Caryl	1948-59	9, 150, 308
Montgomery, James	1923	42
Scottsboro Boys	1931-50	10, 11, 131, 148, 176, 222, 233, 281, 306

RELIGION IN THE SCHOOLS

United States		
Board of Union Free School District No. 9, New Hyde Park, N.Y. Engel v. Board of Union Free School District No. 9	1958	176
Engel, Steven I., et al. Engel v. Board of Union Free School District No. 9	1958	176

RELIGIOUS LIBERTY

India		
Shahidganj Mosque, La- hore, India		104
Ireland		
Sheridan, Edward (Dr.)	1811	221

RIOT

United Kingdom		
Bangor: Bishop of Bangor, et al.	1796	92v.4

Dalrymple, Charles John,
 et al.   1838   243, 246
Edinburgh University
 Students' Riot <u>see</u>
 Dalrymple, Charles
 John, et al.
United States
 Alley, John, Jr.   1822   181v. 14
 Buffum, Jonathan   1822   181v. 14
 Cuming, Samuel   1799   302
 DeCoster, Ezekiel, et al.   1825   181v. 12
 Duane, William, et al.   1799   181v. 7, 302
 Gilman, Winthrop S. ,
  et al.   1838   181v. 5
 Horton, Andrew, et al.   1825   181v. 12
 Moore, Robert   1799   302
 Scott, John, et al.   1817   181v. 7
 Shaw, Benjamin   1822   181v. 14
 Solomon, John, et al.   1838   181v. 5
 Sprague, Preserved   1822   181v. 14

ROBBERY
France
 Aga Khan: Begum Aga
  Khan Jewel Robbery   1953   252
 Cartouche, Dominique   1721   99, 279
 D'Anglade (M. & Mme.)   1687   279
 Lecca, Paul, et al.   1953   252
 Maubreuil: Marquis de
  Maubreuil   1817   171
 Watson, Lindsay George
  (Lt. Col.)   1953   252
India
 Khan, Said   1949   103
 Laxmiprasannamamma,
  Yellamanchilli, et al.   1951   63
United Kingdom
 Biggs, Ronald Arthur   1964   111
 Brodie, Deacon   1788   36, 143, 239, 244
 Great Train Robbers <u>see</u>
  Biggs, Ronald Arthur
 Grey, George, et al.   1956   101v. 3
 Harley, Robert Paul, et
  al.   1938   15
 Hawkins, Robert (Rev.)   1669   51, 73

ROBBERY (cont.)
Mackcoull, James	1820	240v. 2, 247
M'Daniel, Stephen	1755	280v. 4
Parsons, William	c. 1760	51
Ramensky, Johnny	c. 1965	21
Swanson, Maurice	1974	21
Young, Mary	1740	33

United States
Brettinger, Rudi	1950	227
De Pietro, Joseph	1953	54
Fahy, William	1924	54
Great Plymouth Mail		
Robbery	1968	12
Hall, Eli H.	1865	181v. 5
Kelley, John J. see		
Great Plymouth Mail		
Robbery		
Kenniston, Laban & Levi	1817	181v. 14
Kretske, Norton I.	1953	54
McCarthy, Justin William	1948	251
Murray, James	1924	54
Sprague, Charles	1849	181v. 4
Sutton, William Francis	1952	251

SABOTAGE
Soviet Union
Metropolitan Vickers Co.	1933	307v. 1
Monkhouse, Alan, et al.	1933	307v. 1

SEARCH AND SEIZURE
United States
Mapp, Dollree
Mapp v. Ohio Supreme		
Court	1961	306

SEDITION
India
Abdullah, Sheikh Mohammed	1946	214
Azad, Maulana Abul Kalam	1922	214
Gandhi, Mohandas Karam-		
chand "Mahatma"	1922	104, 214
Tilak, Bal Gangadhar	1908	214

Ireland
Davitt, Michael, et al.	1879	43

SEDITION (cont.)
  United Kingdom

Douglas, Neil	1817	71v. 2
Gerrald, Joseph	1794	71v. 2
Macleod, Gilbert	1820	71v. 2
Margarot, Maurice	1794	71v. 2
Mead, William	1670	125
Muir, Thomas	1793	71v. 1, 134, 245
Palmer, Thomas Fyshe	1793	71v. 1
Penn, William	1670	65, 125, 229
Skirving, William	1794	71v. 1

  United States

Debbs, Eugene Victor	1918	295v. 7
Hutchinson, Anne	1637	62v. 1, 208
O'Hare, Kate R.	1917	181v. 13
Penn, William	1690	281
Reynolds, James (Dr.)	1799	302
Stokes, Rose Pastor	1918	181v. 13
Vallandigham, Clement L.	1863	181v. 1

SEDITIOUS LIBEL
  Canada

Jehovah's Witness Appeal	1952	168

  India

Besant, Annie	1916	104

  United Kingdom

Bastwick, John (Dr.)	1637	284v. 1
Baxter, Richard	1685	229, 284v. 1
Burton, Henry	1637	284v. 1
Carlile, Richard	1819	59
Cobbett, William	1810	37
Curll, Edmund	1727	284v. 1
Cuthell, John	1799	92v. 4
Frost, John (1750-1842)	1793	92v. 2
Hatchard, John	1817	284v. 1
Most, Johann	1881	48v. 1
Peltier, Jean Gabriel	1803	48v. 1, 65
Prynne, William	1637	284v. 1
Shipley, William Davis (Dean of St. Asaph)	1784	92v. 1
Stockdale, John	1798	92v. 2
Tooke, John Horne	1777	284v. 1
Wilkes, John	1763	148
Wolseley, Sir Charles, et al.	1820	48v. 2
Woodfall, Henry Sampson	1770	284v. 1

SEDITIOUS LIBEL (cont.)
  United States

Callender, James Thomas	1800	133, 181v. 10, 302
Cooper, Thomas	1800	181v. 10, 302
Crosswell, Harry	1803	181v. 16, 281
Haswell, Anthony	1800	181v. 6, 302
Lyon, Matthew	1798	181v. 6, 302
Zenger, Peter	1732	10, 11, 62v. 1, 98, 177, 181v. 16, 200, 208, 229, 268v. 7

SEXUAL OFFENSES
  United Kingdom

Adamson, John Michael	1978	21
Jocelyn, Percy (Bishop of Clogher)	1822	44v. 2
Wilde, Sir Oscar	1895	10, 11, 129, 132, 293

SOLICITATION OF CHASTITY
  United Kingdom

Fitzroy, Sir Almeric	1922	149

SUFFRAGE
  United Kingdom

Wilks, Mark	1912	295v. 10

  United States

Anthony, Susan B.	1873	181v. 3, 295v. 10
Jones, Beverly W., et al.	1873	181v. 3

TARIFF CASES
  United States

Brancusi, Constantin Brancusi v. U. S. Customs	1927	3
U. S. Customs Brancusi v. U. S. Customs	1927	3

TAX EVASION
 United Kingdom
  Wilks, Mark   1912 295v. 10
 United States
  Capone, Al   1931 55, 257, 258
  Morgan, J. Pierrepoint 1933 258

TORTURE
 United Kingdom
  Picton, Thomas (Gov. of
   Trinidad)   1806-10 33, 48v. 1, 148,
               284v. 2, 292

TREASON
 Belgium
  Cavell, Edith   1915 10, 11
 Canada
  Fenian Invaders   1866 127
  Lynch, Robert Bloss
   "Colonel"   1866 127
 France
  Antoinette, Marie see
   Marie Antoinette
  Bolo Pascha   1918 1
  Caillaux, Joseph   1918 1
  Damiens, Robert Francis 1757 34
  Dreyfus, Alfred (Maj.) 1894-99 10, 11, 38, 82, 111,
               114, 148, 171,
               200, 271, 293,
               305
  Duval   1918 1
  Lenoir, Pierre   1918 1
  Louis XVI (King of France) 1793 11, 44v. 2
  Malvy, Louis Jean   1917 1
  Marie Antoinette (Queen
   of Louis XVI of France) 1793 37, 44v. 2, 293
  Ney, Michel (Marshal) 1815 293
  Quien, Gaston   c. 1915 1
  Toque, et al.   1918 1
 Germany
  Reichstag Fire Trial 1933 82, 307v. 1
 Greece
  Socrates   399 BC 10, 11, 34, 82, 148,
               194, 200, 271,
               293

TREASON (cont.)
  Hungary
    Mindszenty, Joseph (Card.)   1949   11, 305
  India
    Bokhari, Attaullah Shah   1939   103
    Indian National Army
      Trial   1945   194, 214, 262
    Singh, Raja Lal   1846   214
    Zafar, Bahadur Shah   1858   214
  Ireland
    Emmet, Robert   1803   48v. 1, 200, 268v. 5
    Sheares, Henry & John   1798   89v. 1
  Mexico
    Trotsky, Leon   1937   11
  Netherlands
    Barneveldt, Jan van Olden   1619   261
  New Zealand
    Pere, Hamiora   1869   289
  South Africa
    Phillips, Lionel, et al.   1896   81
  Soviet Union
    Moscow Trials   1936-38   82
    Shcharansky, Antoly   1978   305
  Spain
    Ferrer, Francisco   1909   11
  United Kingdom
    Baillie-Stewart, Norman
      (Lt.)   1945   38
    Bateman, Charles (Dr.)   1685   221
    Boleyn, Anne (Queen of
      Henry VIII of England)   1536   87, 129, 310v. 1
    Brandreth, Jeremiah, et
      al.   1817   48v. 2
    Buckingham: Duke of
      Buckingham see Staf-
      ford, Edward (Duke of
      Buckingham)
    Campion, Edmund   1581   310v. 1
    Casement, Sir Roger   1916   17, 36, 87, 111, 148,
                                                 164, 216, 260,
                                                 293, 297
    Cato Street Conspiracy   1820   33, 44v. 2, 48v. 2,
                                                 87, 171, 229
    Charles I (King of England)   1648   10, 11, 37, 44v. 1,
                                                 82, 87, 129, 148,
                                                 171, 197, 280v. 1,
                                                 293, 310v. 1

Despard, Edward Marcus
    (Col.)   1803   48v. 1, 50
Devereux, Robert (2nd
    Earl of Essex)   1600   164, 280v. 3, 310v.1
Essex: Earl of Essex
    see Devereux, Robert
    (2nd Earl of Essex)
Fawkes, Guy, et al.   1606   11, 87, 310v. 1
Fifth Monarchy Rebellion   1660   310v. 2pt. 1
Fraser, Simon (12th Baron
    Lovat)   1746   164, 197
Frost, John (d. 1877)   1840   229, 286v. 1
Fuchs, Claus   1950   111
Garnet, Harry   1606   310v. 1
Gerard, John   1654   310v. 1
Goodman, John   1641   310v. 1
Gordon, George (Lord)   1781   92v. 1
Gunpowder Plot see
    Fawkes, Guy, et al.
Hadfield, James   1800   92v. 4, 163
Hardy, Thomas   1794   92v. 2
Hensey, Florence (Dr.)   1758   52, 221
Hewet, John (Dr.)   1658   310v. 1
Horne, John see Tooke,
    John Horne
Howard, Catherine (Queen
    of Henry VIII of Eng-
    land)   1542   87, 284v. 1
Howard, Thomas (4th
    Duke of Norfolk)   1572   310v. 1
Jackson, William (Rev.)   1795   52
Jesuit Trials   1578-85   310v. 1
Joyce, William   1945   87, 139, 260, 293,
                                                    295v. 9
Lee, Thomas (Capt.)   1600   280v. 3
Lilburne, John   1649   78, 310v. 1
Lincoln, Ignatius Timothy
    Trebitsch   1916   94
Lisle, Alice (Lady)   1685   2, 44v. 1, 87, 125,
                                                    129, 164, 280v.1
Lord Haw-Haw see
    Joyce, William
Lovat: Lord Lovat see
    Fraser, Simon (12th
    Baron Lovat)
The Luddites   1813   48v. 2

TREASON (cont.)

Lynch, Arthur Alfred	1903	260
March: Earl of March see Mortimer, Roger (Earl of March)		
Mary (Queen of Scots)	1586	11, 36, 44v. 1, 129, 148, 194, 287, 293, 310v. 1
Messenger, Peter, et al.	1668	310v. 2pt. 1
Monmouth: Duke of Monmouth see Scott, James (Duke of Monmouth)		
More, Sir Thomas (St.)	1535	87, 284v. 1, 293, 305
Mortimer, Roger (Earl of March)	1330	87
Norfolk: Duke of Norfolk see Howard, Thomas (4th Duke of Norfolk)		
Nunn May, Alan	1946	111
O'Brien, William Smith	1848	286v. 1
Oxford, Edward	1840	33, 286v. 1
Paine, Thomas	1792	92v. 1
Parrott, George Charles	1913	17
Peacham, Edmund	1614	310v. 1
Penruddock, John (Col.)	1655	284v. 1, 310v. 1
Perrot, Sir John	1592	310v. 1
Popish Plot	1678-81	261, 310v. 2pt. 2
Raleigh, Sir Walter	1603	44v. 1, 75, 87, 129, 171, 194, 280v. 1, 293, 310v. 1
Ramsay, David	1631	310v. 1
The Regicides	1660	171, 280v. 1, 310v. 2pt. 1
Russell, William (Lord)	1683	44v. 1, 280v. 2
Scott, James (Duke of Monmouth)	1685	37
Seymour, Edward (Duke of Somerset)	1551	310
Slingsby, Sir Henry	1658	310
Somerset: Duke of Somerset see Seymour, Edward (Duke of Somerset)		
Stafford, Edward (Duke of Buckingham)	1522	310v. 1

Stone, William   1796   92v. 3
Strafford: Earl of Straf-
   ford see Wentworth,
   Thomas (Earl of Straf-
   ford)
Stuart, Mary see Mary
   (Queen of Scots)
Thistlewood, Arthur, et
   al. see Cato Street
   Conspiracy
Throckmorton, Sir
   Nicholas   1554   87
Tone, Theobold Wolfe   1798   284v. 1
Tonge, Thomas, et al.   1662   310v. 2pt. 1
Tooke, John Horne   1794   92v. 3
Twyn, John, et al.   1663   44v. 1, 310v. 2pt. 1
Vane, Sir Henry   1662   310v. 2pt. 1
Wakeman, Sir George
   (Dr.)   1679   221
Watson, James   1817   48v. 2
Wentworth, Thomas (Earl
   of Strafford)   1641   36, 44v. 1, 87, 148,
                                              268v. 7

United States
   Ambrister, Robert C.   1818   181v. 2
   Andre, John (Maj.)   1780   44v. 2, 62v. 2,
                                              181v. 6, 235

   Axis Sally see Gillars,
      Mildred
   Bayard, Nicholas (Col.)   1702   37, 62v. 1, 181v. 10
   Best, Robert   1948   264
   Brown, John (Capt.)   1859   89v. 2, 98, 133,
                                              181v. 6, 208,
                                              235, 271, 281
   Burr, Aaron (Sen.)   1807   133, 208, 281, 287
   Chandler, Douglas   1947   264
   Cook, John E.   1859   181v. 6, 268v. 4
   Coppoc, Edwin   1859   181v. 6
   Cramer, Anthony   1942   177
   Dorr, Thomas Wilson   1844   181v. 2
   Fries, John   1799-   181v. 11
                                 1800

   Fries, John see also
      Northampton Insurgents
   Gillars, Mildred   1948   264
   Gruber, Jacob (Rev.)   1819   181v. 1

TREASON (cont.)
    Haupt, Hans Max, et al.   1942-44   58
    Hodges, John   1815   181v. 10
    Leisler, Jacob   1691   62v. 1, 181v. 10
    Marks, Conrad   1800   181v. 11
    Mitchell, John   1795   181v. 11
    Northampton Insurgents   1799-   302
        1800
    Rosenberg, Julius & Ethel   1951-53   10, 11, 55, 149,
                176, 227, 293,
                303
    Smith, Joshua Hett   1780   62v. 2, 181v. 6
    Sobell, Morton   1951   11
    Toguri, Iva   1949   264
    Tokyo Rose see Toguri,
      Iva
    Vigol, William   1795   181v. 11
    Villato, Francis   1797   302
    Western Insurgents   1795   181v. 11, 302
    Whisky Insurgents see
      Western Insurgents

UNLAWFUL OATH
    Ireland
      Adams, Francis   1832   205
      Langton, Thomas   1832   205

WAR CRIMES
    Germany
      Goring, Hermann   1946   129
      Grese, Irma   1945   189, 227, 266v. 2
      Kramer, Joseph   1945   266v. 1
      Nuremburg Trials   1945-46   10, 11, 82, 98, 111,
                151, 200, 278,
                301, 305
      Nuremburg Trials see
        also Names of Indivi-
        dual Defendants
    Israel
      Eichmann, Adolf   1961   9, 10, 11, 257, 305
    Philippines
      Yamashita, Tomoyuki
        (Gen.)   1945   304

Singapore
   Sumida Haruzo (Lt. Col.)   1946   278
United States
   Calley, William L. (Lt.)   1970   84, 257, 300, 304
   Henderson, Oran (Col.)   1971   300
   Medina, Ernest L. (Capt.)   1971   13, 300
   My Lai Massacre see
     Calley, William L.
     (Lt.); Henderson, Oran
     (Col.); Medina, Ernest
     L. (Capt.)

WATER RIGHTS
  Germany
   Arnold the Miller
    Arnold the Miller v.
     Baron von Gersdorf   c. 1750   287
   Von Gersdorf (Baron)
    Arnold the Miller v.
     Baron von Gersdorf   c. 1750   287

WILLS
  Australia
   Mackie, Grace
    McMeckan v. Mackie   1891   156
   McMeckan, John
    McMeckan v. Mackie   1891   156
  Canada
   Belaney, Archivald Stans-
    field see Grey Owl
    Estate Suit
   Grey Owl Estate Suit   1939   168
  United Kingdom
   Allcard, Mary
    Allcard v. Skinner   1887   315
   Skinner, Hannah
    Allcard v. Skinner   1887   315
  United States
   Anderson, John: John
    Anderson Will Case   1885-91   295v. 4
   Hill, Anthony J. : Anthony
    Hill Will Contest   1953   91
   Jumel, Eliza B. : Eliza
    Jumel Will Case   1866   68

WILLS (cont.)
    Rice, William Marsh:
        Wills of W. M. Rice   1900   295v. 2
    Rothko, Mark: Mark
        Rothko Estate Suit   1974   3
    Russell, John: John Rus-
        sell Will Case   1896   268v. 7
    Stewart, Alexander T. :
        A. T. Stewart Will
        Case   1876   295v. 2
    Wendel, John Gottlieb:
        Wendel Claimants   1932-35 295v. 2

WIRE-TAPPING
    United States
        Berger, Ralph   1966-67 306

WITCHCRAFT
    France
        Gaufridy, Louis   1611   279
    United Kingdom
        Bury St. Edmunds Witch-
          craft Trials   1665   65, 229, 284v. 2
        North Berwick Witches
          Trials   1590-91 247
        Paisley Witches Trial   1697   247
        Suffolk Witches   1665   280v. 1
        Weir, Jean   1670   240v. 1, 244, 249
        Weir, Thomas (Maj.)   1670   240v. 1, 244, 249
    United States
        Bishop, Bridget   1692   181v. 1, 182
        Burroughs, George   1692   181v. 1, 182
        Good, Sarah   1692   182
        Martin, Susanna   1692   182
        Proctor, John   1692   182
        Salem Witchcraft Trials 1692   10, 11, 62v. 1, 82,
                                       235

        Salem Witchcraft Trials
          see also Names of
          Individual Defendants

MISCELLANEOUS (Offenses which
could not be classified under
standard subjects)

AIDING SLAVES TO ESCAPE
  United States
    Walker, Jonathan   1844   181v. 3

ASSUMING POWER OF GOVERN-
MENT
  United Kingdom
    Council of Madras   1780   92v. 4
    Stratton, George, et al.
      see Council of Madras

CORRUPTION IN GOVERNMENT
  France
    Stavisky Inquiry Commis-
      sion   1934   307v. 2
  United Kingdom
    Clive, Robert (Lord)   1722   299

ESCAPING FROM SLAVERY
  United States
    Burns, Anthony   1854   181v. 5

INCITING BLACKS TO CRIME
  United States
    Ury, John   1741   181v. 1

INCITING INDIANS TO RIOT
  United States
    Arbuthnot, Alexander   1818   181v. 2

OBSTRUCTING THE MAIL
  United States
    Gill, Charles   1818   181v. 2
    Hart, John   1817   181v. 12
    Mordecai, Noah M.   1818   181v. 1

REFUSING PAPER MONEY
  United States
    Wheeden, John   1786   181v. 4

MISCELLANEOUS (cont.)
SABBATH BREAKING
   United States
     Neet, Joseph   1899   181v. 14

TEACHING BLACK CHILDREN
TO READ
   United States
     Douglas, Margaret   1853   181v. 7

THREATENING LETTERS
   United Kingdom
     Johnson, Mary (Mrs.)   1912   70
   United States
     Ravara, Joseph   1793   302

VIOLATION OF STATE LAW
REGARDING FISH OIL
   United States
     Judd, Samuel   1818   181v. 3

Bixley, William. The Guilty and the Innocent; My Fifty Years at the Old Bailey. New York: Philosophical Library, 1967. 176p.

Black, Henry Campbell. Black's Law Dictionary. Fifth Edition. St. Paul: West, 1979. 1,511 p.

Dictionary of American Biography. Published under the auspices of American Council of Learned Societies. New York: Scribner, 1964, 11 v.

The Dictionary of National Biography. Founded in 1882 by George Smith. Edited by Leslie Stephen and Sir Sidney Lee. From the Earliest Times to 1900. (With Supplements Covering the Years 1901-40.) London: Oxford University Press, 1949-53. 26 v.

Duke, Thomas Samuel. Celebrated Criminal Cases of America. San Francisco: Barry, 1910. 657 p.

Dunning, John. Truly Murderous; Horrific Modern European Murders Reconstructed. Introduction by Colin Wilson. Blandford: Harwood-Smart, 1977. 226 p.

Gribble, Leonard Reginald. Famous Judges and Their Trials; A Century of Justice. London: Long, 1957. 192 p.

Nash, Jay Robert. Almanac of World Crime. Garden City, N.Y.: Anchor, Doubleday, 1981. 452 p.

Nash, Jay Robert. Look for the Woman: A Narrative Encyclopedia of Female Poisoners, Kidnappers, Thieves, Extortionists, Terrorists, Swindlers & Spies from the Elizabethan Times to the Present. Edited by George C. DeKay. New York: Evans, 1981. 416 p.

O'Donnell, Bernard. The Old Bailey and Its Trials. New
    York: Macmillan, 1951. 226 p.

Sifakis, Carl. The Encyclopedia of American Crime. New
    York: Facts on File, 1982. 802 p.

United States. Library of Congress. Library of Congress
    Subject Headings. Ninth Edition. Washington, D. C. :
    Library of Congress, 1980. 2 v.

Walker, David M. The Oxford Companion to Law. Oxford:
    Clarendon, 1980. 1, 366 p.

Webster's Biographical Dictionary. Springfield, Mass.: Mer-
    riam, 1980. 1, 697 p.

Wilson, Colin. A Casebook of Murder. New York: Cowles,
    1969. 288 p.

Wilson, Colin, and Pat Pitman. Encyclopaedia of Murder.
    New York: Putnam, 1962. 576 p.